TOKENS OF TRUST

TOKENS OF TRUST

An Introduction to Christian Belief

ROWAN WILLIAMS

CANTERBURY
PRESS
Norwich

© Rowan Williams 2007

First published in 2007 by the Canterbury Press Norwich
(a publishing imprint of Hymns Ancient & Modern Limited,
a registered charity)
13–17 Long Lane London EC1A 9PN

www.scm-canterburypress.co.uk

Third impression

British Library Cataloguing in Publication data

A catalogue record for this book is available
from the British Library

978 1 85311 803 6

Designed and typeset by Vera Brice

Printed and bound in Singapore by
Tien Wah Press

CONTENTS

INTRODUCTION

In the early centuries of the Christian Church, one of the most important jobs for its leaders was to prepare people for initiation into its life. Usually this happened at Easter, in a solemn night-time ceremony involving stripping off your clothes, being immersed in water and anointed with oil. In the weeks leading up to Easter, the local bishop would have been giving intensive instruction in what belief meant, the climax of a process of preparation that might have taken a couple of years.

Well, we don't do it quite like that today. But the period before Easter is a good time to think about the essentials of what Christians believe as they get ready for the greatest celebration of the year. And it was with this in mind that I decided to offer some talks in Canterbury Cathedral, in the week before Easter 2005, that might give an outline of what it was all about. This book is a slightly enlarged version of what was said in those talks.

I have tried to keep some of the conversational style of the talks; and I have also tried not to take too much for granted about what readers might or might not know about the Bible or the Church's history. Some of the people who came to the talks in the Cathedral were regular churchgoers in search of a refresher course, but some were fairly new to it all, and I hope they didn't feel that I was assuming they knew more than they did. So I must ask the reader who does know a lot about it to be patient if I explain the obvious.

For example: there are plenty of quotations from the Bible, and the reader will ideally need to have one handy and to know that the 'Old Testament' or 'Hebrew Scriptures' is the record of how God dealt with the (Hebrew-speaking) tribes of ancient Israel over a period of well over a thousand years; and that the 'New Testament', the 'Christian Scriptures', contains the four Gospels, giving the outlines of the life of Jesus, and a lot of letters to newly founded Christian communities around the eastern Mediterranean by senior leaders of the first generation. Most are by Paul, a man who had been a violent opponent of Christianity and had a famously dramatic conversion; others are by people about whom we don't know much but who are still very close to the historical beginning of it all and to the people who'd known Jesus.

Basic to everything here is the idea that Christian belief is really about knowing who and what to trust. I shall be suggesting that Christianity asks you to trust the God it talks about before it asks you to sign up to a complete system. I hope it may become clear how, once you have taken the step of trust, the actual teaching, the doctrine, flows out of that. A good and sensible bit of Christian teaching is good and sensible because it has grown out of exploring the implications of believing in a completely trustworthy God.

So all through these chapters, I'm assuming that we are not just talking about ideas in their own right, but about the interaction between thinking, doing and praying out of which the statements of belief originally came. These statements, mostly held in common between all major Christian bodies in the world, took shape in the first three hundred years of the Church's history, and have shown themselves remarkably tough and durable in all the problems the Church has been through. You'll find the text of the two oldest and most widespread of these 'creeds' (from the Latin for 'I believe') at the beginning of the book.

The pictures are one way of helping you to read a bit more slowly and meditatively. Some of them are by the great twentieth-century poet, painter and engraver, David Jones; he has a way of producing a picture that seems to invite you into a much deeper world by the mysterious lightness of the strokes and the colours. And I hope that one effect of Christian believing is always seeing the world in a new way – seeing beyond the surface without letting go of what's actually there on the surface (which still matters immensely).

The other pictures are simply of some of the people who make sense of the words by their lives. If the sketch of faith I've written here rings any bells, it will be mostly because you will have met people like this, trustworthy people who themselves show how to live in the real physical world while opening up the depths of things. These photographs are meant to remind you of such folk, to tell you that there are those who make sense of it all in this living way.

I'm very grateful to everyone who has helped with turning the talks into a book: Sarah Williams and Jonathan Jennings who looked after the recording and transcribing, Christine Smith of Canterbury Press who encouraged me to think of making a book out of what emerged, Jonathan Goodall, Linda Foster and Mary Matthews who helped so much with editing and checking. And thanks also to all those who turned out to listen in the Cathedral, who stayed through the week (and stayed to pray and listen to music after each evening's session) and who responded so patiently and generously to the whole experience. This book is specially for all of them, and for all God's people in Canterbury.

ROWAN WILLIAMS
All Saints, 2006

The Apostles' Creed

I believe in God the Father almighty,
maker of heaven and earth:
and in Jesus Christ his only Son our Lord,
who was conceived by the Holy Ghost,
born of the Virgin Mary,
suffered under Pontius Pilate,
was crucified, dead, and buried.
He descended into hell;
the third day he rose again from the dead;
he ascended into heaven,
and sitteth on the right hand of God
the Father almighty;
from thence he shall come to judge the quick and the dead.
I believe in the Holy Ghost;
the holy catholic Church;
the communion of saints;
the forgiveness of sins;
the resurrection of the body,
and the life everlasting.
Amen.

The Apostles' Creed, as it appears in the Book of Common Prayer
Morning and Evening Prayer services (1662)

The Nicene Creed

I believe in one God the Father almighty,
maker of heaven and earth,
and of all things
visible and invisible:
And in one Lord Jesus Christ,
the only-begotten Son of God,
begotten of his Father before all worlds,
God of God, Light of Light,
very God of very God,
begotten, not made,
being of one substance with the Father,
by whom all things were made;
who for us men and for our salvation
came down from heaven,
and was incarnate by the Holy Ghost of the Virgin Mary,
and was made man,
and was crucified also for us under Pontius Pilate.
He suffered and was buried,
and the third day he rose again
according to the Scriptures,
and ascended into heaven,
and sitteth on the right hand of the Father.
And he shall come again with glory

to judge both the quick and the dead:
whose kingdom shall have no end.
And I believe in the Holy Ghost,
the Lord and giver of life,
who proceedeth from the Father and the Son,
who with the Father and the Son together
is worshipped and glorified,
who spake by the prophets.
And I believe one catholic and apostolic Church.
I acknowledge one baptism for the remission of sins.
And I look for the resurrection of the dead,
and the life of the world to come.
Amen.

Niceno-Constantinopolitan Creed as it appears in
the Book of Common Prayer Communion Service (1662)

Tokens of Trust

David Jones The Waterfall, *Afon Honddu Fach* (1926)

ONE

Who Can We Trust?

I believe in God the Father almighty

A few years ago, the British philosopher, Onora O'Neill, argued in some broadcast lectures that our society was suffering from a crisis of trust. I suspect we may not need a professional philosopher to tell us the bare fact: pretty well everyone will recognize the sort of thing she means. But it helps to have an analysis of this condition. It isn't simply that we have become remarkably cynical in many of our attitudes, that we approach people in public life with unusual levels of suspicion. It's also, more disturbingly, that we don't feel the great institutions of our society are working for us. This means we are unhappy and mistrustful about our educational system, our health care services and police – let alone our representatives in government. But this is hardly something unique to us. Elsewhere we sense ourselves caught up in international economic and political patterns we can't control and which we don't believe work for our advantage. If we have noticed how things are beyond our national boundaries, we may feel that it's a system that simply doesn't work for human beings in general:

rightly or wrongly, 'globalization' is often seen as a development that takes power away from actual local communities and individuals. And the stories that emerge from time to time about enormous frauds and endemic corruption in some big companies or banks do nothing at all to help. Belatedly, people are writing long books about the need for ordinary human trust and relation-building in business life, and it's very welcome. But the damage has been done, alas; we have learned to be suspicious.

There's no doubt that suspicion can be good for us in many circumstances. We need an edge of critical response in any democracy, and it is healthy that we don't passively take for granted what we're told. But in the UK Baroness O'Neill and a good many others are suggesting that things have gone rather further than this, to the point where we just *assume* that things aren't arranged for our benefit. And when we feel powerless in the face of that, it isn't healthy. Mistrust is always connected with this sense of not being in control, of someone else pulling the strings. And this is a key to why it is such a problem. I feel mistrustful when I suspect that someone else's agenda and purpose has nothing to do either with my agenda or with what that someone else is claiming. They have a hidden advantage; I am being undermined. If I can't see quite how it all works but suspect that something hostile is going on all the same, the effect can be not only humiliating but paralysing. Trust will feel like risk and folly.

There's quite a bit more to say about this, and we'll be coming back to the crises of our society later on; but I want to begin with the question of trust and its absence because the opening words of the Christian statements of faith, the creeds, are about just this. This doesn't always appear straight away, though. We say, 'I believe in one God, the Father almighty, maker of heaven and earth'. The form of words might initially remind us of questions like, 'Do you believe in ghosts?' or 'Do you believe in UFOs?' – questions about something 'out there' whose existence is doubtful, where the evidence is hotly disputed.

But, although there are unfortunately many, both believers and unbelievers, who treat the words like this, this wasn't at all what they originally meant. In John's Gospel (the ninth chapter), Jesus asks the blind man he's just cured whether he 'believes' in the Son of Man. He's certainly not asking (as he might ask about the Loch Ness monster) whether the man is of the opinion that the Son of Man exists; he wants to know whether the former blind man is ready to *trust* the Son of Man – that is, Jesus in his role as representative of the human race before God. The man – naturally – wants to know who the 'Son of Man' is, and Jesus says that it is him; the man responds with the words, 'I believe'.

He believes; he has confidence. That is, he doesn't go off wondering whether the Son of Man is out to further his own ends and deceive him. He trusts Jesus to be working for him, not for any selfish goals and he believes that what he sees and hears when Jesus is around is the truth. Hence the radical difference from 'believing' in UFOs or the Loch Ness monster. To believe in these doesn't make that much difference to how I feel about myself and the world in general, and it has nothing to do with whether the Loch Ness monster is reliable or not. If it existed, it would undoubtedly be useful to know if it was a creature of dependable and regular habits, but that isn't what we have in mind when we talk about believing in it.

The words at the beginning of the Creed, in contrast, do make a difference in how the world feels and you feel. They are closer to the formula used by Buddhists when they make a statement of faith: 'I take refuge in the Buddha' – the Buddha is where I belong, the Buddha is what I have confidence in to keep me safe. And the Creed begins to sound a little different if we begin here.

'I believe in God the Father almighty' isn't the first in a set of answers to the question, 'How many ideas or pictures have I inside my head?' as if God were the name of one more doubtful thing like UFOs and ghosts to add to the list of the furniture of my imagination. It is the beginning of a series of statements about where I find the anchorage of my life, where I find solid ground, home.

Now it may be worth adding a word about one detail before moving on. Some texts start 'I believe', some start 'We believe'; for example, the wording of some of the new services replaces the former with the latter at Holy Communion, and this has caused some controversy. But the fact is simply that the creeds originally had more than one purpose. The shorter text, the Apostles' Creed, was probably used at baptism, the longer and more complicated text, the Nicene Creed, was worked out by councils of church leaders to try and rule out various faulty ideas. So it isn't surprising that the Apostles' Creed begins 'I' – it's a formula for an individual taking a step of commitment in baptism, just like the Buddhist phrase I quoted above – and the Nicene Creed (in its early forms, though it was changed later) begins 'We' – it's a statement of what has been agreed by a meeting and is to be said by the whole congregation together. It won't really do to say that 'we believe' is a general formula that allows individuals more latitude in what they individually sign up to: it sets out what Christians can expect each other to take for granted. You might even say that it tells us why we can trust each other in the Christian community. We're looking in the same direction, working with the same hopes and assumptions. So both 'I' and 'we' have their place, and not a great deal hangs on which of them we use at any moment.

But now to the hard question: *why* should we put our confidence in God the Father almighty, maker of heaven and earth? Have we grounds for thinking him trustworthy? On the face of it, we might almost say that we had reasons for feeling rather unconfident. Surely God, above all, is one whose purposes we can't fathom, whose 'agenda' is hidden from us, a completely alien intelligence, remote and transcendent? The sad truth is that a great deal of religion gives just that impression. God's mysterious ways are appealed to when we can't understand things (especially painful and shocking things), and we are encouraged to think about the vast gulf that separates us from God. But the Bible strongly suggests that this sort of religion is

Why should we put our confidence in God the Father almighty, maker of heaven and earth?

what we have to grow out of. Bad religion is about not trusting God, trying to avoid God or even outwitting him; about approaching

God as 'the management', or the head teacher, perhaps, a presence that is at best critical or hostile, always to be outmanoeuvred where possible.

The Bible gives us various answers to the question of why we should trust the maker of heaven and earth and not regard him as an unfathomable alien intelligence. One of the plainest answers is that found in the Letter to the Ephesians in the New Testament, where the long and complex introductory passage (including one of the longest sentences in the Bible) culmi-

Bad religion is about not trusting God, trying to avoid God or even outwitting him.

nates in the claim that, in the events around Jesus Christ, God has at last made his purpose clear; he has revealed the mystery hidden for ages past, he has shown us what his agenda is. What once was mysterious – or at least shadowy – has now emerged into daylight, and the purposes of God that existed from the world's

foundation are now laid bare for us. Because of Jesus we can now see that what God has always meant to happen is – to pick up two centrally important words in the Letter to the Ephesians – peace and praise. This and this alone is God's 'agenda': the world he has made is designed to become a reconciled world, a world in which diverse human communities come to share a life together because they share the conviction that God has acted to set them free from fear and guilt. And this in turn is only one facet of a reconciliation that somehow affects the whole cosmos, that draws the diversity of the created world itself together so that it works harmoniously. This reconciliation liberates human voices for praise, for celebrating the glory of the God who has made it possible and has held steadily to his purpose from the beginning. This is what God is after, and there is no hidden agenda, nothing is kept back.

Not that this tells us all we could know of God, let alone all there is to know about God. It does not exhaust the sense of mystery or wonder at this 'strange design', as one of Charles Wesley's hymns calls it. It simply assures us that we now know what God's aim in creation is; and it is an aim directed entirely towards the benefit of ourselves and the rest of creation; it is in no way a 'selfish' purpose. God has no reason for deceiving us. If the purpose has been hidden, it is not because God has arbitrarily decided to keep us in the dark. The revelation has to wait until the time is ripe, until the perfect vehicle of communication has appeared. Up to that point, we are still obstinately wedded to various fantasies about God and about ourselves in relation to God. For the first generation of Christians, it was also true that there were spiritual forces around in the universe who had a vested interest in persuading us to think falsely about God – diabolical and deceptive powers who are out to enslave us by creating fear and suspicion towards the Creator. Now they have been shown up, and God himself has communicated his purpose by the life and death and resurrection of Jesus.

So we don't get to know what God is 'like' in the abstract; we don't get a definition delivered in the language of ideas. We get a life that shows us what God wants to happen, one that makes it possible for what God wants actually to become real in and for all of us (just what this might mean is something we shall be coming back to later). We shall never get to know God as God knows God, and our human words will always fall immeasurably short of his reality; God

God cannot be for us an object at the mercy of our scrutiny, because God is always active, never just there over against us like objects in this world.

cannot be for us an object at the mercy of our scrutiny, because God is always active, never just there over against us like objects in this world. The very activity of our thinking minds is what it is because God is activating them here and now. But precisely because we get to know God in what he does, not as an idea or an object, what we discover is his active will – what he wants, what his purpose, his longing is. And because of Jesus, we can understand that longing in terms of peace and praise.

Some of you may remember the great words towards the end of the medieval *Revelations of Divine Love* by the fourteenth-century hermit, Julian of Norwich. She is asked, does she want to know the Lord's 'meaning' in all these visions – does she want to know what his purpose is? And the answer is, 'Love was his meaning'. T. S. Eliot, who knew this text so well, wrote:

> Love is the unfamiliar name
> Behind the hands that wove
> The intolerable shirt of flame
> That human power cannot remove.[1]

At the heart of the desperate suffering there is in the world, suffering we can do nothing to resolve or remove for good, there is an indestructible energy making for love. If we have grasped what Jesus is about, we can trust that this is what lies at the foundation of everything.

You don't have to be a great theologian to notice that this leaves some immense questions unanswered. Some of these we shall have to spend more time on. But at this point, the significant thing is just to see the kind of answer that one of the writers in the Bible gives to the question, 'Why should we trust the maker of heaven and earth?'

However, there is another level at which the question can be answered, connected with what we have just been thinking about but going a bit deeper. In a nutshell, this is about saying that we can trust the maker of heaven and earth precisely because he *is* the maker of heaven and earth. And this isn't simply an appeal to the idea that God must know what he's doing because he's in charge. It says something, yet again, about the character of God.

We can trust the maker of heaven and earth precisely because he is the maker of heaven and earth.

God is the unique source of everything. Therefore, there is nothing God is forced to do. There is nothing alongside God, nothing by nature extra to God or beyond God. God is never one thing among others. So there can be no question of God having to do anything at all that he doesn't want to do. And because he cannot need anything, because he contains all reality eternally and by nature, the only thing that can 'motivate' his action is simply what he is, the kind of God he is. What he *does* shows us what he *is*.

Put slightly differently, this means that God can't have a selfish

11

agenda, because he can't want anything for himself except to be the way he is. So if the world exists because of his action, the only motivation for this that we can even begin to think of is sheer unselfish love. He wants to give what he is to what isn't him; he wants difference to appear, he wants an Other to receive his joy and delight. He isn't bored and in need of company. He isn't frustrated and in need of help.

A word of caution here: some modern thinkers have been very tempted by language that seems to suggest that God is in some way in need of having something else around in order to become more fully himself. And this is tempting because it can sound very chilly if we say that God doesn't 'need' us; surely, when we love and are loved, it matters to know that we are needed. But I think we have to face a challenge here; we must get to grips with the idea that we don't 'contribute' anything to God, that God would have been the same God if we had never been created.

We must get to grips with the idea that we don't 'contribute' anything to God, that God would have been the same God if we had never been created.

In terms of the inevitable give and take of human relationships, this would be a bit abnormal. But God, remember, isn't a reality on the level of anything else. In him is all he could need for his own happiness. And thus we have to bend our minds around the admittedly tough notion that we exist because of an utterly unconditional generosity. The love that God shows in making the world, like the love he shows towards the world once it is created, has no shadow or shred of self-directed purpose in it; it is entirely and unreservedly given for our sake. It is not a concealed way for God to get something out of it for himself, because that would make nonsense of what we believe is God's eternal nature.

God is, in simple terms, sublimely and eternally happy to be God, and the fact that this sublime eternal happiness overflows into the act of creation is itself a way of telling us that God is to be trusted absolutely, that God has no private agenda. It may be a bit shocking and hard to absorb, but that's what it seems we have to say. When – rather rarely – in our world we see someone acting without any thought for themselves, without reward or consolation, wholly focused on another, we see a faint reflection of what God is naturally like.

God is, in simple terms, sublimely and eternally happy to be God.

From one point of view, the difficulty is that we might quite like to think that we were loved because we were nice and helpful to God. But this is a bit like imagining that God forgives us because we're good (rather than making us good by forgiving us, as the Bible claims). The love God shows, in creating us as much as in saving us, is completely free. He doesn't owe us anything. He has chosen that we should exist and he has chosen to treat us always as lovable – as it has been forcefully expressed: 'he has thought that we were worth dying for'. So as soon as we begin to get the notion of creation into focus, we are faced with this demanding insight about unconditionally generous love; and we can perhaps see why there is no ground here for suspicion, no need to step back and say, 'Wait a minute: what's in this for you?'

When we think about the Creator, we ought to have our natural suspiciousness checked at the very root; here at least we have reason for confidence.

As we shall see repeatedly, this belief in God the Creator doesn't unfold by a tidy process of argument. There really is a chicken and egg aspect to it. Human beings encounter God as the one who forgives them without condition and so they start reflecting on the freedom and power of his love. They see the existence of the whole universe in that perspective and come to develop the conviction that 'Love was his meaning' in everything. Or again, human beings are struck silent by the immensity and complexity of the universe, and they dimly start thinking about what concentration of unlimited energy would have to be imagined as holding it all in being; and so they understand more fully why God doesn't treat us according to our deserving, following rules and conditions in his love towards us. What we say about God as maker of everything and what we say about God who meets us personally in forgiveness and renewal ought to be as closely allied as possible; it is one of the failings of some kinds of teaching, I think, that creation and salvation are treated as completely different topics, whereas the Bible seems again and again to hold them inseparably together.

So: I trust, I have confidence in, I take refuge in, the God who has made everything and so can have no selfish purpose and has made visible for us the sort of God he is and the sort of purpose he has in the life and death and resurrection of Jesus. And in this light we can perhaps make sense of the words 'Father almighty'. As they stand, they offer a field day for Freudian analysis: isn't this the clearest possible example of wish fulfilment – to have an all-powerful father to look after me? Wouldn't we all like to have an authority figure who could sort out all our problems, who is always there on hand to help us out of situations where we would otherwise have to take responsibility? And isn't this a fantasy that is deeply dangerous for anyone who wants to grow up as a human being?

The answer to that has to be 'yes'. But it should drive us to ask more carefully just what we mean by the almightiness of God. It has always been tempting to think of it in terms of what *we* would like so as to overcome our limitations – the ability to get whatever we desire, to resolve our own and everyone's difficulties by a flick of the wrist. Given that fantasy, it isn't surprising that people from time to time produce various sorts of comic riff on the theme, in which we are actually put into what we imagine is God's position and discover that – of course – it isn't so easy (the recent film *Bruce Almighty* comes to mind). But if – once again – we pay a bit of attention to how the language of the Bible and Christian practice works, we might discover that this sort of fantasy is nothing to do with it. If 'I believe in God the Father almighty' means 'I believe that there is somewhere an unlimited power that can choose and perform anything it likes, and I need to be on the right side of it', that doesn't sound as though it had much to do with trust; an almighty power like that, a huge arbitrary will, could be very unsettling indeed.

The word translated 'almighty' in fact in the Greek means 'ruler of everything' or even something like 'holder of everything'; and this suggests a slightly different approach. It means that there is nowhere God is absent, powerless or irrelevant; no situation in the universe in the face of which God is at a loss. Which is much the same as saying that there is no situation in which God is not to be relied upon. The freedom of his love which we have been thinking about, implies that his love never exhausts its resources, whatever may happen in the universe in general or in my life in particular. There will be more to say about this later on, in a number of different contexts, but for the moment simply bear in mind the ways in which we can get the idea of 'almightiness' a bit wrong by thinking of it in terms of a great wish-fulfilment fantasy instead of seeing it as a way of saying that God always has the capacity to do something fresh and different, to bring something new out of a situation – because nothing outside himself can finally frustrate his longing. So almightiness in this sense becomes another reason for trust.

God always has the capacity to do something fresh and different, to bring something new out of a situation.

What the Bible puts before us is not a record of a God who is always triumphantly getting his way by doing miracles (we'll be thinking about miracles in the next chapter), but a God who gets his way by patiently struggling to make himself clear to human beings, to make his love real to them, especially when they seem not to want to know, or to want to avoid him and retreat into their own fantasies about him. And typically, the Bible sometimes does this by a very bold method – by telling a certain kind of story from the human point of view, as if God needed to be persuaded to be faithful to his people. Someone like Abraham or Moses, someone who has good reason to know something about what God is really like, is faced with a crisis. Things are going badly; surely God is going to give up and blast people into oblivion. So Abraham and Moses argue with God until they have persuaded him to be merciful. The writers of these stories knew exactly what they were doing. They didn't believe in a bad-tempered, capricious God who needed to be calmed down by sensible human beings. They knew that the most vivid way of expressing what they understood about God was to show Abraham and Moses appealing to the deepest and most true thing about God as they pray to him.

So in the first book of the Bible, in chapter 18 of Genesis, Abraham is arguing with God about God's plan to destroy the wicked city of Sodom. Surely, says Abraham, there must be *some* good people in Sodom. And if there are, 'the judge of all the earth' must be fair to them; he can't destroy the good with the bad: 'far be it from you to do that!' says Abraham. And God lets himself be bargained with, as Abraham haggles away, gradually reducing the number of good people there would need to be in the city for God to spare it. It's a story about a man who is discovering, bit by bit, that God really is to be trusted to do right, not to be unjust.

Even more poignantly, in the second book of the Bible, chapter 32 of Exodus, there is the story of Moses arguing with God. Moses has been on the mountain top, receiving the commandments from God; meanwhile, in the camp of the people of

Israel, his brother Aaron has been persuaded to make an image of God in the shape of a golden calf. God's anger is aroused, and he tells Moses to 'let him be', and he will destroy the whole rebellious mob and start again with Moses alone as the ancestor of a new nation. And Moses replies by saying, in effect, 'You can't do that; you have promised to be faithful to *this* people. Do you want the rest of the world to say that you couldn't cope with them after all, that you couldn't keep your promises?' And, he goes on a bit later in the same chapter, 'if you won't forgive them, don't make an exception of me: blot my name out of your book as well'. It's as if Moses is saying, 'I don't want to be involved with a God who changes his mind and isn't capable of forgiving and starting again with the same old sinful and stupid people.' What matters to Moses isn't his own safety and his own future; what matters is that the God he has believed in is still the same, still trustworthy because he sticks with sinful, stupid people and so demonstrates the absolute freedom of his love. If God were to tear up his promises to Israel, it would look as if his love were just conditional on their good behaviour. But instead there is this miraculous vision of a God who can still do something with this appallingly unpromising material.

It sounds as though the ancient Hebrews really understood the difference between a God who could do whatever he liked and damn the consequences and the God who had shown himself to them as a God of commitment and forgiveness, ready to be argued with, ready to be 'recalled' to his true nature by those who really understand him. The stories are, in one way, tongue in cheek. They invite us into precisely the fantasy we've been thinking about: what would *you* do faced with the wicked city, faced with the disastrous stupidity of the people of Israel in the desert? You'd be very tempted to annihilate them, wouldn't you? Well, that's the difference between you and God, and between false gods and real ones; *this* is what almightiness looks like in practice. It's the unlimited power to be there, to be faithful to and for a world that is deeply unstable and unjust and suspicious and uncooperative: the power to go on trying to get through at all costs, labouring and wrestling with the human heart.

This is why belief, trust, in God the Father almighty is so different from wish-fulfilment and projection about some all-powerful character who can just do what he decides and get what he wants straight away. Instead it's the discovery of what Abraham and Moses have discovered, a God who never runs out of love and liberty. And although I shall have a lot more to say about the meaning of the word 'Father' when we come to concentrate more on what Jesus tells us of God, we already have more than a glimmer of understanding about it in these

God is to be trusted as we would trust a loving parent, whose commitment to us is inexhaustible, whose purposes for us are unfailingly generous.

stories. God is to be trusted as we would trust a loving parent, whose commitment to us is inexhaustible, whose purposes for us are unfailingly generous; someone whose life is the source of our life, and who guarantees that there is always a home for us. So perhaps we can park Freudian fantasies of all-powerful fathers for a moment. If there's a problem here, it may be almost the opposite – that we can risk projecting on to God the character-istics of an idealized mother, always accepting and soothing. That we need to free ourselves from that fantasy is something we shall be considering later. For now, what matters is to grasp the idea of a God whose power is made clear in his patience and his capacity always to bring something fresh into a situation. And again we can begin to see why the execution of Jesus could seem to the first Christians not a defeat but a decisive moment of divine power.

In the last part of this chapter, I want to turn to an issue that is going to be around quite a bit in Chapter 2: how can we know that any of this is actually *true*? So far, I've been trying to clarify what the words mean. But how does anyone ever get inside this lan-guage, get to the point where they can make it their own? Christians may be talking about a trustworthy God, but how do we know that this is a real God, as opposed to an impressive char-acter in a book? In other words, does God exist?

You won't be surprised to hear that I haven't yet found the deci-sive new argument that will prove once and for all that there really is a God; but we do need to remember that the number of people who come into a living personal faith as a result of argument is actually rather small. Many centuries ago, a great theologian and pastor, St Ambrose, said that 'it did not suit God to save his peo-ple by arguments'.[2] Of course they have their uses. When people argue against the existence of God, it helps to have some points you can make to counter the idea that belief is just completely irrational. But what is it that shifts people's imagination and vision and hope?

The Bible has no arguments for the existence of God. There are moments of conflict with God, anger with God, doubt about God's purposes, anguish and lostness when people have no real sense of God's presence. The Psalms are full of this, as is the Book of Job. Don't imagine that the Bible is full of comfortable and reassuring things about the life of belief and trust; it isn't. It is often about the appalling cost of letting God come near you and of trying to trust him when all the evidence seems to have gone. But Abraham, Moses and St Paul don't sit down to work out whether God exists; they are already caught up in something the imperative reality of which they can't deny or ignore. At one level, you have to see that the very angst and struggle they bring to their relation with God is itself a *kind* of argument for God: if they take God that seriously, at least this isn't some cosy made-up way of making yourself feel better.

Faith has a lot to do with the simple fact that there are trustworthy lives to be seen.

And that is actually quite a serious point about where belief in God starts for a lot of folk. It starts from a sense that we 'believe in', we trust some kinds of people. We have confidence in the way they live; the way they live is a way I want to live, perhaps can imagine myself living in my better or more mature moments. The world they inhabit is one I'd like to live in. Faith has a lot to do with the simple fact that there are trustworthy lives to be

21

seen, that we can see in some believing people a world we'd like to live in.

It puts quite a responsibility on believing people, of course. It would be much nicer for all of us if we could just rely on arguments, not on the uncertainties of human lives. But nonetheless, the remarkable fact remains. Some do take responsibility for making God credible in the world. This turn of phrase, about taking responsibility for God, I owe to one of the most striking believers of the twentieth century, one of the many who made God believable by their resistance to the nightmares of modern totalitarianism and violence. Etty Hillesum was a young Jewish woman in her twenties when the Germans occupied Holland – not a pious or conventional person at all, not someone with an explicit religious commitment. Her published diaries and letters from 1941 to 1943 show how, during this terrible period in the history of her country and her people, she became more and more conscious of God's hand on her life, at a time when most would have been likely to feel more deeply sceptical about God.

Imprisoned in the transit camp at Westerbork, before being shipped off to Auschwitz where she was to die in the gas chambers in November 1943, at the age of twenty-nine, she wrote, 'there must be someone to live through it all and bear witness to the fact that God lived, even in these times. And why should I not be that witness?' In a letter to a friend from Westerbork, she described her life as having become 'an uninterrupted dialogue with You, oh God', and she could write of sensing her vocation in the camp as being 'not . . . simply to proclaim You, God, to commend You to the heart of others. One must also clear the path toward You in

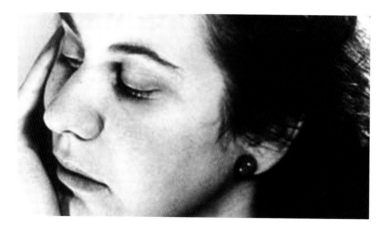

Etty Hillesum: witness to God on the road to Auschwitz

them'.[3] It is plain that she saw her belief as a matter of deciding to occupy a certain place in the world, a place where others could somehow connect with God through her – and this not in any self-congratulatory spirit or with any sense of being exceptionally holy or virtuous, but simply because she had agreed to take responsibility for God's believability.

Of course it is a story from exceptional times – though, with the recent histories of genocide in our minds, we shouldn't imagine that they were as exceptional as they should be, and there are no doubt parallel records and stories from Rwanda or Sudan to be told. What makes Etty Hillesum special is hard to say exactly. It's worth noting that one of the people she met briefly in the Westerbork camp was Edith Stein – a distinguished philosopher of Jewish background who had become a Catholic and then an enclosed nun. Her order had moved her from Germany to try and save her from the Nazi genocide, but the invasion of Holland had caught up with her. She too was to die in Auschwitz. Now she is recognized as a saint of the Roman Catholic Church. Much could be written about her witness, in her writings and in her death, not least in her willingness to die with her own people despite her conversion to Christianity. She is in every way a more obviously and conventionally holy person than Etty Hillesum, and a very great woman by any possible definition. But there is something about Etty's human passionateness, her bohemian energy and indiscretion and the slow and surprising character of her journey towards God that speaks to those of us who find it harder to be at home in religious institutions of any sort.

Extreme situations do make things clear. And if it is possible to take responsibility for God's credibility on the road to Auschwitz, that is a contribution – whether it comes from a Carmelite nun or an irrepressible young writer and teacher – to the sum total of human possibilities that cannot easily be written off. Even in less dramatic situations, though, we can see something of what it means to make yourself responsible for God. One of the surprise best sellers in the USA a couple of years ago was a book entitled *Father Joe: The Man who Saved my Soul.*[4] Tony Hendra was one of the scriptwriters for *Spitting Image*, probably the most uninhibitedly scurrilous and outspoken satirical programme on British television in the 1980s; in his book, he describes his friendship from the age of fourteen with a Benedictine monk, Father Joseph Warrilow, a man who had become a monk at the age of eighteen and had hardly ever left his monastery on the Isle of Wight. Over decades, Father Joe remains a point of utterly reliable orientation for Hendra, accessible and compassionate all the way through crises of faith, successes, failures, marriage and divorce and remarriage, problems with drugs, attempted suicide. He never tries to score points or win arguments; he is supremely himself, faintly comic and completely unselfconscious in appearance and manner, as steady as granite in his insight and his love. He patiently recalls Hendra to who and what he really is, time and again, puncturing illusions and ambitions.

The slow healing of Hendra's second marriage and his return to the Catholic faith are presented not as dramatic success stories but as the result of an unfailingly truthful presence in his life:

Father Joe:
friend and
conduit
to God

'Father Joe's wisdom, like the correct medication for a long mis-diagnosed illness, began to have its effect', he writes about this process. He describes Joe as 'a saint of what could be done . . . a saint of imperfection' – a man who always started where God started, with the rather sad and shopsoiled reality which God seeks to make glorious. And when he finally opens his adult heart again to Joe, Hendra says, 'Like a tidal wave overwhelming the breakwaters of common sense came the thought that this slowly shrinking, mud-flap-eared old elf of a man was . . . God. Or a body God would from time to time inhabit.'[5]

'But I didn't believe in God', adds Hendra instantly. 'Father Joe would connect it for me, somehow, sometime.'[6] This is a relationship in which – in a much less tragic and extreme situation than that of Etty Hillesum, though tragic enough in terms of human suffering and doubt – someone has become responsible for God, for making a connection that argument and speculation cannot make. I suspect that for many believers something not unlike this is going on a good deal of the time. We may be uncertain, still racked by doubt and inner anguish, we may be unable to give any very satisfactory account intellectually of what we believe; but somewhere in our horizon there are people who make the connection. Never mind that such people may themselves often be almost as anguished or struggling as we are: the point is that what we see is someone who is a native of the world in which we want to belong. Cardinal Newman once said that a magnifying glass can kindle a fire somewhere else even if it remains cold in itself.

Quite a lot of religion – and
this is particularly so in England – seems to depend on a grateful
awareness that someone else is doing it for you. Whole books have
been written about how the physical presence of church buildings
and cathedral choirs performs a vital social job in giving us somewhere to put our feelings of dependence and need. So many people are glad that *someone* is committed even if they're not sure
they themselves want to be.

It's easy to make fun of this, and some Christians find it
maddening. But it isn't complete nonsense. It suggests that many
of us are becoming aware of dimensions in our humanity that are
not properly looked after by any of the
things that are normally supposed to make
us feel all right. And if people are on the way
to some bigger recognition, perhaps they
need to go at their own speed and in their
own way. They have to work out whether
they really have enough confidence in those
who are 'taking responsibility for God' to
make them take the final step of belonging.
And when they can do that, then they begin
to discover something of what is involved in
fully believing.

Many of us are becoming aware of dimensions in our humanity that are not properly looked after by any of the things that are normally supposed to make us feel all right.

Of course there is a choice that can't be
avoided eventually, a choice to take the risk
and see if you can really be at home in the

It's a choice that may be helped a bit by intellectual discussion but is seldom, if ever, settled by it.

world of an Etty or a Joe. It's a choice that may be helped a bit by intellectual discussion but is seldom, if ever, settled by it. And when belief is rather weak in a society (like ours), the not very welcome question for believers, not least those who are supposed to hold positions of leadership and teaching authority, is whether we look remotely trustworthy. Often all we can do is to go on telling the stories of those who keep *us* going; I may not look very credible, but I can at least point to someone who does. And as long as there are those who effectively and bravely take responsibility for God, the doors remain open and the possibility is there for others, perhaps very slowly, to find their way to a point where they can say, 'I believe'. Not just, 'I'm convinced that there is something called God' (on its own, that's too like believing in UFOs), nor even, 'I'm convinced that believers are talking about something real' (though that's a step in the right direction, and one that is often connected with the presence of trustworthy, credible people around), but the ultimate choice, 'I want to live in the same world as them; I want to know what they know and to drink from the same wells.' That's when we can truly say, 'I believe; I have confidence; I take refuge; I have come home.'

DAVID JONES The Waterfall,
Afon Honddu Fach (detail)

DAVID JONES The Annunciation, *Y Cyfarchiad i Fair* (1963)

TWO

The Risk of Love

maker of heaven and earth

It's all very well to appeal to the significance of lives lived in such a way as to point us to God – you might say; but you still haven't tackled the basic question of why we should take the language of God seriously in the first place. It may well be that, once you've taken it on board in some way as a possibility, lives like the ones we have just been thinking about bring it alive. But what if you can't find a way into the language at all?

This is usually where arguments for God's existence begin to appear on the screen – understandably so, and we need to spend a bit of time looking at what they claim to offer. But before this, it is just worth noting that what no argument for the existence of God has ever tried to do is to deliver a full-blooded account of what conscious personal *relationship* with God actually amounts to; and so they all fall some way short of introducing us to the essence of faith. It is perfectly possible to come to the end of an argument for God's existence and to say, 'So what?' It is less easy to read Etty Hillesum's letters and say, 'So what?'

Arguments for God's existence invite us to look at the world as a single whole – to look at the sum total of all the processes we can think of as actual and possible and to ask, 'Is there a way of making sense of them *as a whole*?' For quite a lot of people, including plenty of modern philosophers, this is not a question that can usefully or even meaningfully be asked. The sum total of all actual and possible processes is just that, the sum of a lot of things each of which can be made sense of in its own terms. You don't need an explanation of the whole thing because there isn't a 'whole thing'. Yet two factors seem obstinately to stick around and create difficulties for those who take this view. One is the stubborn intuition in most people that it is a fair question to ask where it all comes from; the other is the general trend of scientific research towards the notion of a 'first event', a point from which the universe as we know it begins to expand. Neither of these is conclusive as a trigger for talking about God, or anywhere near a knockdown argument. Yet there remains this nagging awareness of a question that it is hard not to ask.

In Tom Stoppard's brilliant play, *Jumpers*,[7] George, the philosophy professor, is preparing a lecture on God's existence for his class and uses the memorable phrase, 'If there is an apparently endless line of dominoes knocking itself over one by one . . . somewhere there was a domino that was *nudged*.' That idea is crude in itself, but it does express the suspicion that if we talk about things in motion, it is hard to avoid a question about what first moves them. In a scientific climate where the fundamental categories have to do with energy and movement, the question of what *energizes* is a very plausible one. We can put it another way. Our universe is a fantastically complex network of different sorts of 'arrangements' of energy; no specific form is basic or unchangeable, yet energy is always conserved. Why, if every specific form of active existence is going to stop being what it is and turn into something else, is there never a moment when the entire network collapses into incoherence, into complete randomness? We recognize randomness at the smallest, most primitive level of existence, yet the big picture is never random. Just what is it that holds the balance, that makes what we encounter a true *universe*, a bounded, self-consistent, interdependent system?

It is not nonsense to say, 'These questions are out of order; all we can possibly say is that this is how it is.' But many are still haunted, and this is one of the areas where it is at least possible to suggest to people how the notion comes in of the whole universe being related to a reality that does not stand alongside it but somehow holds or includes it, a reality that is simply action, movement, without any restriction or qualification. You may just be able to see here how this sort of talk connects with what we were thinking about in the last chapter in relation to God's freedom. If all we meant by 'God' was a bigger and better agent within the same system, a higher stage of explanation but still within the same universe, we'd still need further explanation (that's why schoolchildren go on asking, 'If God made the world, who made God?'). Religious philosophers have tried to avoid this by insisting that when we get to the stage of referring to God, we are no longer talking about levels of explanation within the same system; we're trying to get our minds around the idea of an activity that is so utterly consistent with itself, so unaffected by any other activity, that it is, so to speak, its own explanation, its own 'cause', eternal and unchanging.

More on that in a moment. Time for a word or two of caution. This is not the same as saying that God, at some time in the past, started the world off and then let it develop. The Roman Catholic writer and journalist Alice Thomas Ellis, in one of her wonderfully acid and witty and poignant novels, imagines someone saying that she thinks of God as a frightfully brilliant academic who published his great work of genius long ago and is now in retirement. And sometimes that caricature is not too far from the way some have spoken of these things. In the eighteenth and nineteenth centuries, thanks to a cleric called William Paley, one of the favourite analogies was that of the watch and the watchmaker. If you are walking on a remote country road and find a watch lying around, you don't conclude that it's a rare species of rural plant life; you take it for granted that it was made by a watchmaker. The world is a hugely complex reality, and we need to think of a creating mind to explain it, rather than supposing it 'just growed', as Topsy in *Uncle Tom's Cabin* explained her origins.

But this analogy doesn't really help us much, if at all. The one thing belief in a creator doesn't say, in Jewish, Christian and Muslim tradition, is that God made the world and then stood back and left it lying around, so to speak. Believers in all these religions would say that creation is going on *now*. There is indeed a beginning point, but it is the beginning of an active relationship that never stops. For God to create is for God to 'commit' his action, his life, to sustaining a reality that is different from him, and doing so without interruption. If I might offer an analogy that is probably as bad in its way as

Creation is going on now.

the watchmaker image, think about an electric light burning. The electric current *causes* the light to shine, but that doesn't mean that the electric power is something that was around only at the moment you put the switch on, so that the light itself is a rather distant result. On the contrary, the light is shining here and now because the electric current is flowing here and now. In the same way, it is the 'current' of divine activity that is here and now making us real.

It should be a rather exhilarating thought that the moment of creation is now – that if, by some unthinkable accident, God's attention slipped, we wouldn't be here. It means that within every circumstance, every object, every person, God's action is going on, a sort of white heat at the centre of everything. It means that each one of us is already in a relationship with God before we've ever thought about it. It means that every object or person we encounter is in a relationship with God before they're in a relationship of any kind with us. And if that doesn't make us approach the world and other people with reverence and amazement, I don't know what will.

Each one of us is already in a relationship with God before we've ever thought about it.

One of the greatest Christian minds ever,

Thomas Aquinas, said in the thirteenth century that we should never think of creation as an event, with a before and after, or as a change in circumstances – as if first there was a chaotic mess, then God came along and organized it, which was a popular view in the ancient world. Creation is an action of God that sets up a relationship between God and what is not God. Eternally, there is just God – outside time because he doesn't get better or worse, or change in any way. And time begins when God speaks to call into being a world that is different and so establishes a reality that depends on him. It depends on him moment by moment, carried along on the current of his activity. Behind and beneath everything we encounter is this action. We may look at something that seems unmoving and unchanging, like the pillars of a cathedral or the peaks of a mountain, but what is within and beyond it is an intense energy and movement. The scientist, of course, will tell us that at the heart of every apparently solid thing is the dance of the subatomic particles. The theologian ought to be delighted that this sort of talk puts movement and energy at the centre, but will want to add that at the heart of the subatomic particles is an action and motion still more basic, beyond measure and observation – the outpouring of life from God.

> To all life thou givest, to both great and small,
> In all life thou livest, the true life of all

says the hymn ('Immortal, invisible'), and it says it all. There is the real Christian doctrine of creation, creation that is going on as we speak or write or read. It's a vision present in many of our prayers as well as hymns, and it's there too in the Bible, most of all in what are usually called the 'Wisdom Books' of the Old Testament and the Apocrypha – Proverbs, bits of Job, some of the Psalms, the Wisdom of Solomon, the Wisdom of Jesus son of Sirach, and so on. One of its most beautiful expressions is in the seventh chapter of the Wisdom of Solomon, which speaks of God's wisdom as a spirit gentle and keen and peaceful and intelligent, always permeating the universe and always looking for friends and co-operators in the world of human beings, looking for a home in the human mind and heart. And when, in chapter 17 of the Acts of the Apostles, St Paul is talking to the intellectuals of Athens, he quotes approvingly from a Greek poet saying that in God 'we live and move and have our being'.

Keep this in mind and at least *some* of the pointless stand-off between religion and science may get into proper perspective. Faith doesn't try and give you an alternative theory about the mechanics of the world; it invites you to take a step further, beyond the nuts and bolts, even beyond the Big Bang, to imagine an activity so unrestricted, so supremely itself, that it depends on nothing and is constantly pouring itself out so that the reality we know depends on it. Creation isn't a theory about how things started; as St Thomas Aquinas said, it's a way of seeing everything in relation to God. Whatever you encounter is there because God chose that it should be there.

Faith doesn't try and give you an alternative theory about the mechanics of the world.

Problems start looming pretty promptly, of course. It's possible to misunderstand this and think that, if God is at the heart of everything, there is somehow no real difference between God and the world – the view we know as pantheism, 'God equals everything'. The point to remember if this sort of confusion arises is that the difference is between an action (God's) that is caused by nothing outside itself, that is completely independent, and varieties of action that belong together in a system of *inter*-action, interconnection, with everything affecting everything else. God doesn't (and logically can't) 'extend' himself, stretching out like a rubber band or flowing out like liquid; he makes what isn't him and sets up a free and loving relationship with it all. It's not 'inside' him, like the letter in the envelope, and he's not inside it. These aren't relationships in space and time, because space and time come to be when and only when God moves to create (think about the oddity of the word 'when' in that last phrase, and you see the challenge to our intellects that is involved in following this through). If there were no creation, God would be the same God, no less in glory and beauty. God's presence in things isn't like a law of nature; it's the effect of his free decision. Pantheism would be to say that the sum total of all the things there are adds up to God, or that God is simply a universal principle inside it all; Christianity says that the sum total of all that there is is held together by God's action and will, and that God is not 'exhausted' by that – if you took the universe away, there would still be a God no less great than before.

But that still leaves the biggest problem of all – the problem of evil. If the action of God is at the heart of everything, every object, every process, what does that imply about suffering and disaster, about cancers and tsunamis? We need to be clear from the start that we are not going to have an answer to this that allows us to sit back and stop worrying, as if we could say, in response to a tsunami or a landslip, 'That's all perfectly straightforward and no one need have any doubts or misgivings.' If we got to such a stage, we should have become desensitized to the awful immediacy of pain and grief. We should be valuing human lives and human welfare less than we should. There's something about the very anguish of the questioning that illustrates just how seriously we have learned to take human pain – and that seriousness is the best witness to the difference that faith makes. No one is dispensable, no one's suffering is insignificant, just a statistic.

So an explanation that even hinted that some lives were less important than others would be a betrayal of one of the basic insights of faith. But there are a few things that we can at least bear in mind before we decide that talking about God makes no sense at all in a world of terror and disaster. If God makes a world that is really different from him, a world of interaction and interconnection, this means a world that is capable of change. Different processes flow together, mesh together and make things happen. This is a world in which any event has what is practically an unmeasurable range of causes, factors that have made it fall out this way rather than that. If these processes were all programmed never to collide with each other in new and changing ways, the world would just be a set of self-contained little clusters of connected phenomena, guaranteed not to change more than a certain amount. And it's a moot point whether such a world would really be as different from God as it needed to be to have some kind of integrity of its own, some kind of consistency overall as one system, a real *universe*. We have begun to think more seriously in recent years about how even the smallest phenomenon in the world can have a disproportionate and surprising effect (the butterfly's wing in Asia contributing to the whirlwind in Europe). It's hard to give a completely sensible account of a world consisting of lots of systems isolated from each other so that certain kinds of interaction never happen.

It looks as though the very notion of a coherent universe implies that the processes of change won't always be smooth or gradual; there can be cataclysms, 'violent' moments when the interactions are explosive. At certain temperatures, earthquakes occur and volcanoes erupt; at certain temperatures, ice caps melt. If there were no human beings or other living things around, this would not be a problem. But part of the integrity, the interconnectedness, of the world is that its processes have brought life and

Would a world with a perpetual safety net really be a world at all?

intelligence into being. The world of natural processes also now includes beings who can think, plan and choose. It's a world in which human beings have freedom about where they choose to live – and they may opt to live where volcanoes erupt.

Is God to make it impossible for people to live in such places? Or should he always step in with a warning or a miracle when it becomes too dangerous? How bad does it have to be before God steps in? When we get to this point, we may begin to have an inkling that there's something a bit strange

Untameable nature in the volcanic landscape of Lanzarote

about the questions. Would a world with a perpetual safety net really be a world at all, a place with its own integrity and regularity?

This does absolutely nothing to make it emotionally easier to face something like the Asian tsunami, nothing at all; it won't stop us questioning God or protesting to God. But we have to try and keep our heads clear enough to recognize that natural disasters are just that, the laws of nature going ahead. It is unspeakably terrible that people and animals are caught in the flow, so to speak; but can we imagine a world where certain processes were always halted in their tracks by God if there were a risk to living creatures? If the world is not just a veil for God's reality, not just a matter of appearances with no continuity in them, there is no quick way through this. And what makes it possible to find God credible even in this context will not be a knockdown argument explaining why evil occurs but – once again – the experience of how actual people find God real even in the middle of these terrors.

If someone right up against the worst of suffering finds it possible to live honestly with God, this is, as we saw in the first chapter, a kind of witness, a testimony that God can be taken seriously; and we can't just write off the whole thing as self-indulgent nonsense.

Does this mean that God makes a *risky* world? Clearly yes, as we see it; anything that is less than God is exposed to risk. And God takes the riskiness to an extreme point in making a world in which there will emerge creatures with minds and freedom. But if God were to say, 'I'll pour out on the world every aspect of my life and action except freedom', that would be a holding back on God's part that suggests a rather unimpressive picture – a picture of a God who refuses the challenge of *real* difference at its toughest level. God's purpose in creation is to bestow as much of his being and life and joy as is possible – and that includes pouring out his freedom, so that creatures like you and me can live. As the Bible says, creation comes to a sort of climax point when God makes something that reflects him more fully than anything else – beings capable of choice and of love. This 'image and likeness' of God, as the Bible's first chapter puts it, is on a different level from the rest of creation, though still absolutely part of it and its inter-connections. And when this happens, the riskiness and uncertainty built into creation also reaches a new level. The threats to security are not only in natural processes but in human choices – which may be simply stupid or actively hostile to God and to others.

If we were to put it a bit irreverently, the question is whether

God is really *serious* about making a world; because if he is, he will put into it all that he possibly can of his own life without actually pulling it back into himself. So it is appropriate that in the universe there should be beings who show something of God's liberty, God's love, God's ability to make new things and to make relationships. It's just because God does take the universe seriously that there are such risks; this is a complex creation, both coherent and fragile. And if, in the light of this creation, the universe we're actually in, we are challenged to have confidence in its maker, it isn't because he has guaranteed our safety but because he remains

This is a complex creation, both coherent and fragile.

there, accessible and free to move things on, even in the most desperate situations. And some of those closest to the risks are most aware of this presence. In the Old Testament, Job, who has suffered indescribable loss and anguish, says at one point, 'If he kills me, I shall still trust him' (Job 13.15). We can still hear people say something like it today; I don't think we can just ignore them.

All right, you may say, but this is a rather austere picture of how the universe works. Aren't Christians supposed to believe in miracles? Doesn't the Bible give us a clear picture of a God who can impose his will on creation when it suits him? And if the Bible is right, then surely there is justification for the agonized cry that sometimes goes up, 'Why does God intervene there and not here?' Why are some prayers apparently answered and some not? I remember a vivid example from years back, when someone who had been involved in a very upbeat and confident charismatic

*Why does God
intervene there
and not here?*

prayer group asked why God should be thanked for finding parking spaces for members of the prayer group when he couldn't be bothered to sort out the conflict in Northern Ireland.

It's a very good question indeed. If we are to answer it at all, we'll need to think back a bit to what was said in the first chapter about different ideas of almightiness – and to remember the warnings about thinking of God's almightiness in terms of what we might like to be doing if we were almighty, just doing whatever we wanted. I have been trying to suggest the picture of a God whose almighty power is more of a steady swell of loving presence, always there at work in the centre of everything that is, opening the door to a future even when we can see no hope. So how might that apply to the question of miracles?

Well, one thing that tells us is that we can't be doing with the sort of notion of miracles that some seem to have, as if God hearing our prayers were like someone receiving applications. He ticks some and puts a cross by others and hands the forms back for action by some angelic civil service. There is a hint of a slightly more sensible approach in an idea put forward by St Augustine in the fifth century – that miracles were really just natural processes speeded up a bit, 'fast-forwarded'. This may be a bit too simple; but Augustine had got hold of something that many thinkers of the Middle Ages followed through in different ways. If God's action is always at work around us, if it's always 'on hand', so to speak, we shouldn't be thinking of God's action and the processes of the world as two competing sorts of thing, jostling for space.

But what if there were times when certain bits of the world's processes came together in such a way that the whole cluster of happenings became a bit more open to God's final purposes? What if the world were sometimes a bit more 'transparent' to the underlying act of God?

God is always at work, but that work is not always visible. God is always at work, but sometimes the world's processes go with the grain of his final purpose and sometimes they resist. But if certain things came together in the world at this or that moment, the 'flow' would be easier and more direct. Perhaps a

God is always at work, but that work is not always visible.

really intense prayer or a really holy life can open the world up that bit more to God's purpose so that unexpected things happen. We're never going to have a complete picture of how that works, because we don't have God's perspective on it all. But we can say that there are some things we can think, say or do that seem to give God that extra 'freedom of manoeuvre' in our universe. And whether we fully understand what's going on or not, we know that it's incumbent on us to do what we can to let this happen. We pray, we act in ways that have some chance of shaping a situation so that God can come more directly in. It isn't a process we can manipulate; miracles aren't magic, and we could never have a comprehensive manual of techniques for securing what we pray for. It would be very comforting if we knew the formulae for success, but we don't. All we know is that we are called to pray, to trust and to live with integrity before God (to live 'holy' lives) in such a way as to leave the door open, to let things come together so that love can come through.

God, I've said, always has the freedom to keep the door open and to let new things emerge. But we can put ourselves more at the service of this freedom or less; we can give ourselves to it or resist it. And if we hold on to a picture of this kind, it may help a bit in thinking through this question of why some prayers are 'answered' and others are not. It can't be because God likes some people more than others or because some people know the right strings to pull or buttons to press, or because God can be battered into submission by a heavy campaign of praying. You can hear people talking about prayer in terms that suggest that it works like one of those models, but a moment's Christian thought will make it plain that they imply another very silly and unflattering idea of God. All we know is that our prayer or our offering of some act of love or devotion can be one of the innumerable factors in a situation that may shift the balance of events and open the door further.

But surely the miracles of Jesus are more straightforward than that? Yes, in one way, and we should expect them to be; where Jesus is (and we'll have more to say about what this means in the next chapter), there is prayer and holiness in unique intensity, so that the door is always more open in the vicinity of his human reality. The same is true in lesser degrees of many great saints. *But*, even when this has been said, we have to notice that the Gospels don't suggest that he could just do whatever he wanted wherever and whenever. He says himself that people are cured by their trust in him; and when that trust isn't there, he can't do as much. In the fourth chapter of St Mark's Gospel there is a passage that has rather scandalized some Christians, where we're told that in Nazareth Jesus 'could not do many mighty works' because the people were sceptical. Even where Jesus was, not all the factors always came together.

So, although Jesus is sometimes (rather disarmingly) shown in very early Christian painting with something like a magic wand in his hand, a magician is exactly what he isn't. His miracles happen when his own boundless compassion comes fully together with other elements in the situation, and something is released and changed. And those other elements include the trust of the suffering person or, in some cases, of their parents or friends. The miracle is at one and the same time completely the action of God *and* the fruit of making room for God in the world by prayer and confidence and receptivity. And (an important extra) if a miracle doesn't occur, that doesn't necessarily mean that the sufferer has failed to show enough trust or hasn't deserved healing. Awful damage is done to people by some 'healers' who suggest this. It is simply the case that we never fully know how much is altered by prayer, what other circumstances might stand in the way of its fulfilment and so on.

It may be worth adding a word or two about the two most celebrated miracles in the story of Jesus, as they're going to be relevant to the next chapter – the virginal conception of Jesus and the empty tomb, the claim that Jesus' birth was an act of God independently of the usual means of reproduction, and that after his death his body was not in the grave but appeared in transfigured or altered form to his friends. Many people have problems with these. Belief or disbelief in them is sometimes used as a sort of test of full and acceptable Christian orthodoxy. I must admit that I am uncomfortable with this kind of test – simply because there isn't a lot of point in isolating the stories and asking for a yes or no in a vacuum. But I'm equally uncomfortable with those who simply take it for granted that the idea of miracle is empty and indefensible, so that these stories can be no more than metaphors. If we *don't* take this for granted, and if we begin from a robust idea of God's action burning intensely in every moment of the world's existence, always just around the corner of our perception, we may be less inclined to be completely sceptical. Just what would the trust of Mary have had to be like for the door of life itself to open in her body? What must the faith of Jesus and his closeness to God have been that death was unable to close its doors on him and relegate him to the past? These considerations don't, of course, settle the question; but they're worth thinking about as we make up our minds. Believing in these stories doesn't have to commit you to a magical view of miracle, to a God who simply decides, '*Here* I'm going to interfere and *here* I'll let things take their course.'

God has – mysteriously – made a world in which what human beings do can help or hinder what he achieves at any point in the world's history; when we give him space, through our prayerful consent to and identification with what he wants, things may happen that were otherwise unpredictable. A prejudice against any sort of miracle may be a buried uncertainty about the unfailing presence and action of the Creator, about that burning intensity of divine action that is always around us. It may reflect a version of the watchmaker image, a world wound up by God long ago and ticking steadily on, uninterrupted. But that is hard to square with the faith of the Bible and the Christian tradition, according to which we live in a world where God's active presence is both invisible and inscrutable on the one hand, and, on the other, almost unbearably close wherever we are and whatever is happening. The poet William Blake, who had a vision of trees full of angels at Peckham Rye, is a safer guide than William Paley to a world that may not be secure but is pulsing with something unmanageable, terrible and wonderful just below its surface.

That might prompt a few thoughts also about how we actually conduct ourselves in the world. In the Nicene Creed, we say that we believe in a God who creates 'heaven and earth and . . . all things visible and invisible'. The phrase is a helpful reminder that creation is more than we can get our minds around – more than what just happens to be on hand for us. A similar idea occurs in the sixteenth Sura of the Qur'an, which says that God has made creatures for purposes that have to do with us and our welfare *and* creatures about whose purpose we have no idea at all. There is obviously something here that Christians and Muslims – and probably people from other faiths too – can agree about. The world is not simply what we can manage and use for ourselves; there are unfathomable dimensions to it, hidden realities, hidden connections (or connections that we discover only too late, like

The race to consume

the effect of carbon consumption on the atmosphere). Things in the universe exist in relation to the Creator before they exist in relation to us, so that a degree of reverence and humility is appropriate when we approach anything in the created order. Our present ecological crisis, the biggest single practical threat to our human existence in the middle to long term, has, religious people would say, a great deal to do with our failure to think of the world as existing in relation to the mystery of God, not just as a huge warehouse of stuff to be used for our convenience.

God has made what we can see and manage and what we can't see and can never manage, a universe some of which we can get a grasp of and some of which we can't. This isn't a recommendation not to try to understand, but simply a reminder that not everything is going to be made sense of from our point of view. We don't get to the end of being baffled and amazed. I sometimes think that this is the importance of talking about angels in Christian teaching. Odd as it may sound, thinking about these mysterious agents of God's purpose, who belong to a different order of being, can be at least a powerful symbol for all those dimensions of the universe about which we have no real idea. Round the corner of our vision things are going on in the universe, glorious and wonderful things, of which we know nothing. We're so used to sentimentalizing and trivializing angels – they are often reduced to Christmas decorations, fairy godmothers almost (as in most of the extraordinary flood of books about angels in recent years). But in the Bible angels are often rather terrifying beings occasionally sweeping across the field of our vision; they

Things are going on in the universe, glorious and wonderful things, of which we know nothing.

do God strange services that we don't fully see; they provide a steady backdrop in the universe of praise and worship. They are great 'beasts', 'living creatures', flying serpents burning with flames, carrying the chariot of God, filling the Temple in Jerusalem with bellows of adoration, echoing to one another like whales in the ocean. Those are the angels of Isaiah and Ezekiel – anything but Christmas card material. And sometimes a human form appears to give a message from God and something in the event tells the people involved that this is a moment of terror and truth, and they recognize that they have met an angel in disguise.

Now whether or not you feel inclined to believe literally in angels – and a lot of modern Christians have a few problems with them – it's worth thinking of them as at the very least a sort of shorthand description of everything that's 'round the corner' of our perception and understanding in the universe – including the universal song of praise that surrounds us always. If we try and rationalize all this away, we miss out on something vital to do with the exuberance and extravagance of the work of God, who has made this universe not just as a theatre for you and me to develop our agenda, but as an overwhelming abundance of variety and strangeness.

I realize that taking angels seriously probably raises a few eyebrows these days; but it's more than just picturesque fantasy that's at stake. Anything that puts our own human destiny a bit more into perspective isn't a waste of time in this obsessional and addictive age, where we are so tempted to think that if it's nothing to do with me it isn't significant. But I want finally to turn to one further aspect of this belief in a God who is responsible for everything. When the creeds of the Church were written, there were some very popular rival systems around which worked on the assumption that God the Father almighty *hadn't* created heaven and earth. After all (and we might remember our earlier discussion) the world we experience is complicated and in many ways seems dark and dangerous. Some of it is ugly; much of what goes on seems meaningless. Wouldn't it be simpler to say that the world as it is has been made by a not very competent second-class divinity, or that some bits of the world are made by God and some by a hostile or evil power?

Anyone who has ever lived through a summer with large quantities of wasps will quite likely have wondered just what the point is of some really annoying creatures. More seriously, it does seem at first that splitting up the responsibility for creation between different powers could solve the problem of evil quite neatly. These solutions were extremely attractive in the world in which Christianity grew up, and they still have their appeal. So it mattered a good deal to begin the creeds with a clear statement that nothing in the world was the result of an accident or a disaster. As the Bible says in its first chapter, what God made was good; nothing (and no one) is bad by nature. As we've seen, the tensions and collisions between the elements in the world produce situations that we can rightly call bad; but this is the effect of events, not of some 'virus' inside certain things or people that is evil by definition. So the whole range of human experience and natural phenomena and process is of concern to God. There's no kind of thing or person that is objectionable to God by nature or insignificant for God, nothing that isn't his responsibility.

But a God who is only interested in the 'acceptable' bits of our life is going to be a sadly limited God.

As you know very well, I'm sure, the way Christians have talked can sometimes give you the opposite impression. To give the best-known example, so much of what has been said over the centuries about the body and the emotions has strongly suggested that God shrinks from these aspects of our existence and that if we are to please God we have to keep as quiet as we can about them. But a God who is only interested in the 'acceptable' bits of our life is going to be a sadly limited God. It is a terribly risky and challenging thing to say that God is responsible for the whole universe when so much of it poses such agonizing moral and imaginative questions; but I think it's more of a problem to have a God who can't cope with being involved in the full range of reality.

Belief in a Creator of all things visible and invisible is in fact something of deeply practical and personal meaning. It is about the possibility of an *integrated* life – not a life where some bits of us have to be covered up or swept under the carpet. 'Visible and invisible' means something for the life of each one of us, you see. There are the things in my life that I'm aware of, there are the things I'm not aware of – and there are the things that I *try* not to be aware of, that I'm ashamed of or frightened by. But all that I am is the working out of what God has made; some of it has worked out well, some not so well; I have learned to make good use of some of what God has given me and I've made a mess of some of the rest or just haven't come to terms with it. Saying that God has made us in our entirety and is concerned about all of us isn't, incidentally, the same as saying that anything we choose to do is fine – only that every aspect of who we are needs to be brought into the circle of God's light, because he can deal with all of it. And that also means that we shouldn't be surprised if Christians are interested in things like politics or economics, art or sport, and have awkward questions to ask and contributions they want to make. There are no areas that are essentially off-limits if God is truly the Creator of *this* world.

So out of the confused and fearful and partial picture of our-

All that I am is the working out of what God has made.

selves that most of us work with most of the time, God can make some sort of wholeness. He can lead us gently to face what we find unacceptable and learn how to make it meaningful by his grace. He can draw the scattered bits of myself together. He is not going to be bored, disgusted or impatient with anything he has made, even when we have made a mess of it for ourselves. It's in this way that the creating God and the forgiving God belong absolutely together – as our first chapter was implying.

The first phrases of the Creeds are not just about the beginning of the universe. They're about the present state of the universe and the present state of you and me and our society. They express a confidence in the God who can make us one with ourselves and with our world, the God who can take the darkness in us and heal it and turn it towards the light. He can make one meaningful life out of our spirits and our bodies. As we shall see later, the belief in resurrection tells us that what God wants to hold in everlasting life isn't some shadowy fragment of ourselves but the person we have become, body and soul. When we express trust in 'God the Father almighty, maker of heaven and earth, and of all things visible and invisible', we affirm that we have grounds for hoping that our lives, in all their fragmentedness, their conflict and their imperfection, can be held and drawn into cohesion – just as the diverse and alarming world itself is held in cohesion – so that God's own self-consistent active love and beauty may be reflected within the universe. We have grounds for hoping that our lives here within the complex system of created reality can show in some degree the gratuitous and generous love out of which everything comes, the love of the Creator in whose image we are made.

Text within the image: SANCTVS CHRISTVS DE CAPEL·Y·FFIN

DAVID JONES A Man for All Seasons, *Sanctus Christus de Capel-y-ffin* (1925)

THREE

A Man for All Seasons

and in Jesus Christ his only Son our Lord

In the first chapter, we had a glimpse of why Christians talk about a God who can be trusted: this is a God who has made his purpose clear. The life of Jesus of Nazareth, 2000 years ago, was seen by those who were closest to him as the key to God's nature and intentions; it is because of Jesus that we grasp the idea of a God who is entirely out to promote our life and lasting joy. Within a few decades of his crucifixion, it was possible to say that in him 'all the fullness of God was embodied' (Colossians 1.19). Here is a human life so shot through with the purposes of God, so transparent to the action of God, that people speak of it as God's life 'translated' into another medium. Here God is supremely and uniquely at work.

How on earth did such a claim come to be made? It isn't as if the Jewish world of Jesus' day was used to moves like this; there were plenty of people claiming to be, or thought to be, divinely anointed messengers of renewal, but none attracted this sort of language. It isn't even that distance lent enchantment to the view, so that when the real history of Jesus was long-forgotten it became possible to spin strange fantasies around his memory. Some of the most extravagant claims appear in the oldest strands of the New Testament, well within the lifetime and the neighbourhood of those who had known Jesus of Nazareth intimately.

To begin to answer that question, we have to look first of all at an area about which the creeds don't have much to say – the actual work of Jesus in his lifetime as the four Gospels present it to us. What Jesus was remembered as having stressed was that the kingly rule of God was about to arrive and break in to the human world. We were about to learn what it was for God to be king, what it was to live under his rule and no one else's. And Jesus' bold proposal was that living in a world and a community in which God was king was something very simple. To live in this world was what happened when you said 'yes' to what Jesus himself was saying and offering; to live under the kingship of God was deciding to live in the company of Jesus and trusting what he said about God and about you.

Trust this, live in Jesus' company, and you become a citizen of a new world, the world in which God's rule has arrived. You will still be living in the everyday world in which many other powers claim to be ruling; but you will have become free of them, free to co-operate or not, depending on how far they allow you to be ruled by God. And what you do and say will become a sign of what is coming. Your life will give a foretaste of God's rule; and it will be directed to inviting as many as possible to come under the same rule, and to resisting the powers (natural and supernatural) that work against God and seek to keep people in slavery.

The famous text known as the 'Beatitudes' in the fifth chapter of St Matthew's Gospel ('Blessed are the poor in spirit . . .') isn't so much a list of rules to follow; it just tells us what sort of lives show that God is in charge – lives that are characterized by dependence on God's goodness, that show forgiveness, single-mindedness, longing for peace and for justice, and patience under attack. People who live like this already belong in the new world: the kingdom is theirs. And, as this ought to make clear, this message is both a very sharply social and political one, and one that will never be captured by political and social reform alone. The changed life that these texts outline will challenge all sorts of things in our present world, but the change in question is one that can only begin in a personal yes to what Jesus is saying and offering.

In terms of the historical world in which Jesus was speaking, all this was something of real and immediate relevance. The Jews of Jesus' day were acutely concerned about who was going to be a true member of God's people when the great change came and God's rule was fully established. The different Jewish groups all had rival solutions. You could be assured of your belonging if you were obedient to the sacrificial laws and the demands of the priestly class; or if you obeyed the oral law in all its detail; or if you went off to the desert and lived a life of strict ritual purity in community. What Jesus says cuts across this – and cuts across the ritual and legal conditions for belonging that the other groups in different ways take for granted. The revolutionary claim that emerges is that Jesus is proposing to redefine what it means to belong to God's people.

To get a sense of just how revolutionary that was, you have to remember that the Jewish Scriptures repeatedly stress that the people of Israel only exists because of God's call or invitation. If you look at a book like Deuteronomy, the fifth book of the Bible and one of the most important collections of Israel's laws, you'll notice that it underlines the idea that Israel exists as a community simply because God has chosen that it should – because of God's promise and invitation. And now here is a human teacher, Jesus of Nazareth, saying, in effect, 'You will be a people if you accept *my* promise and invitation.' To belong with God, to be a citizen of the new world, is bound up with being committed to Jesus, trusting him, seeing in what he is doing the action of the God of Israel himself, reshaping and refounding the community he has called to be specially his in the world. Where Jesus is at work, healing, forgiving, welcoming people who were not welcome in any of the existing categories of Israelite life at the time – people who were never going to keep all the ritual laws or who had failed to be faithful to the moral law and needed restoration – there is what Jesus himself called 'the finger of God' at work.

More than this again: being in Jesus' company involves growing into a new relationship with God. Jesus' followers ask him to teach them to pray, and he tells them to begin, 'Our Father'. Jesus' friends share with him a relation of intimacy with God, a relationship more like a family relationship than anything else. If you stand where Jesus is standing, you can say what Jesus says; you can come to God as father without going through a lot of complex religious or ritual conditions. To be with him is to be – so to speak – under a clear sky, with no intermediaries between you and the maker of all things. St Paul expresses it a bit later by talking about being 'in' Jesus. He has marked out the place for us all to stand. He has made something new possible, not by pushing himself between us and God but by taking us into his own life and experience. We are not just citizens living under the new government of God; we are adopted into God's intimate family.

Read the Gospels with this in mind, and you can see why there was nothing bland and obvious about Jesus in his own day. Archbishop William Temple once remarked that some sorts of modern theology gave you the impression that Jesus went to Jerusalem to deliver a course of lectures on the Fatherhood of God and the Brother-

There was nothing bland and obvious about Jesus in his own day.

hood of Man (motherhood and apple pie, as it were), and met with an unfortunate miscarriage of justice, quite incomprehensible to us. Who could possibly disagree with his message of love and reconciliation? In fact, the answer is, 'plenty of people' – in his day and ours. Given the explosive political and religious atmosphere in which Jesus worked, the claim to speak on behalf of God so as to create a new people or nation, to establish a new government, and to change the way they thought of their relation with God, was very far from motherhood and apple pie. And what people wanted to say about Jesus himself as a result was a lot more than just respectful remarks about a great teacher.

As we've noted, it doesn't take any time at all for Jesus' followers to be using extravagant language about him. There is really surprisingly little in the New Testament of any stage of early Christian belief when people thought Jesus *just* a teacher or a prophet. And this is because the emphasis is not on the *ideas* of Jesus but on what he has *done*; he is someone who by his action and his invitation has made a measurable difference to the human landscape by creating a new community that prays in a unique way. Faced with this, very few seem to say, 'How interesting'; they tend rather to ask, 'Who on earth is this that we're dealing with? By what right does he say all this?' The world of Judaism in this period was one in which there was plenty of speculation about angelic powers who were granted some share in the glory of God, and who might be expected to appear on earth in the last days in some way or another. And you can see that Jesus immediately attracted some of the language and imagery that belonged in this world of speculation (it's there in the Letter to the Hebrews as well as in Paul's letters and John's Revelation). But even this won't quite do the job. As the New Testament unfolds, you can see writer after writer wanting to go beyond language about angelic powers. If there is some power more than the human at work in Jesus' life, it isn't just that of an angelic grand vizier standing in the presence of God. This is more; this is a power that can make free with all the promises of God as if there were simply no gap between it and God himself.

Awkwardly and slowly and with much complication and even apparent contradiction, the New Testament moves towards the extraordinary notion that the Creator of the universe is at work without interruption in the life and work of Jesus – that it is God who is doing what Jesus is doing. 'He sent no angel to our race/ Of higher or of lower place' says an old hymn – picking up the language of the first chapter of the Letter to the Hebrews about how you had finally to draw a clear line between what was said about angelic powers and what was said about Jesus.

But prayer often runs ahead of ideas. You can see the distinctions gradually getting clearer in the minds of the New Testament writers, but something has long since happened to the heart and imagination. Early in the Acts of the Apostles, the record of the

Prayer often runs ahead of ideas.

first years of the Christian community's existence, St Luke describes the dramatic trial and execution of Stephen, the first Christian martyr; as Stephen dies, he prays, apparently without thinking twice about it, *to Jesus*, 'saying, Lord Jesus, receive my spirit' (Acts 7.59). Just as, in the Gospels, the disciples of Jesus ask, 'Who is this that even the winds and the waves obey him?' or his enemies ask, 'Who is this who forgives sins?' we might ask here, 'Who is this who receives spirits?' When Jesus himself dies, according to St Luke, he commends his spirit to his Father; and now here is Stephen commending his spirit to Jesus. In other words, Christians approach Jesus now as though he were completely with God, associated with God, able to do what God does, and so correctly addressed as if he were God. In the last book of the Bible, the Revelation to John, the series of visions begins with the risen Jesus appearing, and he is greeted by the visionary prophet with the prostrations of worship; later in the book, when the prophet is going to prostrate himself before an angel, he is told off pretty sharply.

The striking thing is how quickly all this fell into place at the level of prayer and imagery, even if the ideas took time to catch up; it is all happening within a time frame no longer than (at most) the period that separates us from the end of the Second World War. Plenty of the evidence shows what happened within a much shorter period of about thirty years. The idea that treating Jesus as divine is a late addition of foreign ('Greek') theories to an original simple message about Jesus as a great teacher who suffered a tragic death is not remotely plausible. The mind-stretching dimension of what is going on in Jesus is there from the start. And it is reinforced by the conviction that drove the friends of Jesus out to foreign lands, to share the news in foreign languages. They were quite sure that what they had to say about Jesus would be equally relevant wherever they went, and whoever they met; you didn't have to be a Palestinian Jew, to speak Greek or Aramaic, to understand.

It's an important point and a surprising one. We can easily forget that in the ancient world there wasn't much of what we'd call 'missionary' activity; religious practice was largely local and ethnic. Some small cults travelled and attracted some success away from their home areas; but no one else in that world was going around insisting that *this* story was potentially everyone's. We know something about how the community associated with Jesus spread into the world of the Greek Mediterranean cities, and to Rome itself and beyond; we know rather less, though still a fair amount, about how missionaries travelled to Persia and India in those very early days. And it's always in the sublime confidence that what they had to say about Jesus would be as challenging and as life-giving there as anywhere else. They saw Jesus as a 'man for all seasons', a man for all climates and languages, capable of transforming any human situation by his presence. And when you put it like that, you can

Jesus . . . is supremely the one who makes God credible, trustworthy.

see how this echoes what is said about God's all-powerful nature, capable of transforming any situation.

Jesus, then, is seen as embodying, making visible, the purpose of God and the action of God; he brings to light peace and praise as our destiny, reconciliation with God and each other – and he makes these things not just visible but possible. He is supremely the one who makes God credible, trustworthy. In his second letter to the church at Corinth St Paul says that all God's promises find their 'yes' in Jesus (2 Corinthians 1.20); he establishes that God's promise is to be trusted.

But there is more still. Yes, Jesus is a human being in whom God's action is at work without interruption or impediment. But wait a moment: the Jesus we meet in the Gospels is someone who prays, who speaks of putting his will and his decisions at the service of his Father. He is someone who is in a relationship of *dependence* on the one he prays to as Father. In him there is divine purpose, power and action; but there is also humility, responsiveness, receptivity. Somehow, the divine presence in Jesus, if it's really a presence in all he does and says, is working itself out in this humility and responsiveness, not just in power as we understand it. And the deeper truth that now begins to swim into focus is that what we understand by 'God' can't just be power and initiative; it also includes receiving and reflecting back in love and gratitude. Jesus (to put it crudely) isn't God just when he's being strong and in control; he's God when he speaks lovingly to God the Father, when he submerges what his human nature fears or longs for in love for the Father. If you take the life of Jesus as a whole, you are prompted to think of God's love as both a giving and a receiving, a flowing out and a reflecting back, an initiative and a depending. Again very early on, the New Testament writers began struggling with this notion of a God whose life was not that of a heavenly individual on his own, but a life of relationship and inner movement and differentiation.

Jesus turned towards the world is God's wisdom and power in action; but Jesus turned towards the Father is the embodiment of a sort of divine response to divine generosity, the Son turned towards the Father. The life of God is not only the outpouring gift, it's a life in which our own response of selfless gratitude and response is also foreshadowed for ever. Jesus is divine responding embodied in our nature and our world; he responds freely and totally to the gift of the Father, and that response is no less divine than the gift – a *perfect* response that is both human and more than human.

It took three and a half centuries for Christians to find words for this that didn't completely break down; and even then, they came up only with a sort of holding formula, not a final theory. Yet already in St John's Gospel, in the really extraordinary first chapter of that work, we see all this outlined (sixty or seventy years at most after the crucifixion). From the beginning, says John, God's living energy is streaming out from him, his mind and purpose, his *logos* (of which 'word' is only a partial translation); and in this energy the world is made. But that living, communicating energy is itself a form of life that is 'in relation' with God – in Greek, *pros ton theon*, literally 'directed towards God'. The mind and purpose of God is crystallized in a form of divine existence that is lovingly and faithfully giving back to God what God has poured out. All that it is is God, yet it is God's loving energy in a new mode, not of giving but of responding. And if you turn to St Paul, you find there, less economically expressed, both the idea of Christ as power and wisdom of God and the idea of Christ as the one who gathers up all things that the Father has made and brings them home to the Father through the work of an eternal love that has worked itself out in time and space (compare chapter 1 and chapter 15 of 1 Corinthians). Jesus Christ, the anointed monarch of God's people, stands at the heart of the twofold movement, of God's life towards the world and the world's journey to reconciliation with God.

So it isn't surprising that the biblical writers aren't content with a scheme that makes Jesus no more than a heavenly power among others. As the writer of the Letter to the Hebrews asks, rather scornfully, did God ever say to any of the angels, 'You are my Son', as he says to Jesus? Jesus truly embodies the absolute eternal love and action of God; but what is so startling and revolutionary, what sets Christian faith apart most decisively from even its closest religious relatives, is this picture of divine life involving receiving as well as giving, depending as well as controlling. It means, among many other things, that we human beings, who live in relationships where we are both givers and receivers, both depending and controlling, can reflect the life of God in every aspect of what we are; we are no less in God's image when we acknowledge our dependence or when we offer thanks than when we are taking decisions or showing God's love to another. That isn't actually an easy message for a world very much in love with the ideal of absolute self-sufficiency – but that's another story. It also means, this surprising and difficult vision, that God never *starts* being in loving relationship; it's an aspect of what he is eternally. Love doesn't begin only when God makes the world.

God never starts
being in loving
relationship;
it's an aspect of
what he is
eternally.

Here, then, is a human narrative – of a skilled artisan from a not very distinguished town in a backwater province occupied by foreign armies, a car mechanic from somewhere near Basra, as we might think of it in contemporary terms; someone who walked the dusty and dirty streets of his town and the lanes of the country, who felt hungry and thirsty, slept and woke, ate and drank, felt ordinary emotions, died. And we are asked to read this story as the story of God's work among us, because this life changes what is possible for human beings and demonstrates once and for all who God is, what God wants, and what God is doing. So the Creed of Nicea, in the fourth Christian century, takes a deep breath and tries to sum up:

> [We believe] in one Lord, Jesus Christ,
> the only-begotten Son of God,
> begotten of his Father before all worlds,
> God of God,
> Light of Light,
> Very God of Very God,
> begotten not made,
> being of one substance with the Father,
> by whom all things were made.

What is alive and at work in Jesus is the first and unique 'product' of divine life, generated by unconditional love quite apart from the existence of the world. And the relation of that unique reality to God the Father is not only like that of child to parent, it is like that of one flame to another from which it has been lit – a favourite image for the early Christians and a very good one still: light one candle from another, and you don't have any less of the first flame and you do have a flame as bright and hot as the first. Light from Light: the Father, the Source, gives all he is and has into the heart of this outflowing 'product', this 'generated' reality, the Son. The Son truly shares the living flame of God's nature with no qualification or lessening, he is 'of one substance' with the Father, his character and nature is to be defined exactly as the Father is

'One equal light': prayer in South Africa

defined. And it is because of this everlasting relationship that there is a world at all – because God is always a God of relation and gift, whether or not there is a universe.

You can see perhaps why this brings us close to the very centre of why we can see God as trustworthy. What God shows himself to be in Jesus is simply what he always is; he doesn't decide to be like Jesus for thirty-odd years or even thirty thousand. God is thus and not otherwise. There is a phrase associated with two of the greatest Anglican thinkers of the last generation, Michael Ramsey and John V. Taylor: 'God is Christlike and in him there is no un-Christlikeness at all.'[8] What is seen in Jesus is what God is; what God is is the outpouring and returning of selfless love, which is the very essence of God's definition, in so far as we can ever speak of a 'definition' of the mystery. The phrase in the Creed, 'being of one substance with the Father' or 'of one being with the Father' can sound a bit chilly and technical – even worse in the form 'consubstantial'. You find it in the last verse of one or two old hymns – 'Consubstantial, co-eternal,/While unending ages run'. Yet it ought to be one of the most exciting words in our vocabulary, telling us that what is happening in the person and activity of Jesus of Nazareth, the workman from the backwater town, is one with the essence of God, and nothing less. I'm sorry to say that some new hymn books alter these words for the benefit of those who can't understand 'consubstantial'; a minor campaign of civil disobedience when faced with the weaker new versions seems called for.

Because God is like this, the world exists. God, you could say, is in the habit of sharing life, pouring out love. He doesn't have to (as if some alien power made him), but it's completely 'in character' for him to make a universe in which he can create more sharers of his love. God, says one ancient theologian, is 'generative' by nature, and if he weren't, there would never be anything but God. God's outpouring of love into the world in the life and death of Jesus is completely continuous with the creation itself and with the eternal truth of the Father's 'generating' of the Son – like one great river in several different landscapes.

No Christian with any sense has ever denied that this is potentially difficult as well as exhilarating to think about. On the one hand we see the human being – the car mechanic, the man who suffers and weeps and sleeps and wakes, vulnerable and mortal; on the other hand we see the act of God, reshaping his chosen community and, through them, reshaping the whole creation – the act

Christian teaching isn't just static; it's always trying to learn from the last set of mistakes.

of God, the Word of power. And we can't pull them apart. As the early theologians of the Greek Church loved to say, it is the same person who weeps for his friend Lazarus and who raises him from the dead – two sorts of life, one of them unconditionally powerful, one utterly vulnerable, but lived inseparably in one person. G. K. Chesterton said his book, *Orthodoxy*, that true Christian teaching was like a vehicle driving very fast down the road, wobbling furiously from side to side yet somehow staying upright – 'reeling but erect'. The process of wobbling is pretty evident in most of our Christian history: sometimes we overemphasize the human Jesus and forget the divine, sometimes (more commonly, perhaps) it is the other way round. But somehow the language and the prayers and the pictures find their balance again and keep going. At least it means that Christian teaching isn't just static; it's always trying to learn from the last set of mistakes.

Christians have used all kinds of images to make clearer the relation between the eternal divine life of the Son or the Word and the human individual Jesus of Nazareth. One image that has helped me a good deal over the years is to think about *music* for a moment. When you see a great performer, a singer or instrumentalist, at work realizing a piece of music, you are looking at one

Jacqueline du Pré

human being at the limit of their skill and concentration. All their strength, their freedom, and you could even say their love is focused on bringing to life the work and vision of another person. Think of Jacqueline du Pré's legendary playing of Elgar's Cello Concerto – memorably captured on film – and you may see what I mean. But you see it any time you go to a concert, classical or popular, when you go to a cathedral service with choristers, when you watch a singer close up on the big screen. Here is someone who is completely themselves, free and independent, and yet for this time the whole of their being, their life, their freedom, their skill, is taken up with this mysterious, different thing that is the work to be brought to life. The vision and imagination of another person, the composer, has to come through – not displacing the human particularity of the performer but 'saturating' that performer's being for the time of the performance.

Now, could we imagine what it might be like for a whole lifetime to be given up to 'performance' in that way? Because that, surely, is what we're trying to say about Jesus as a human being. He is performing God's love, God's purpose, without a break, without a false note, without a stumble; yet he is never other than himself, with all that makes him distinctly human taken up with this creative work. If we look at great musicians, we see both the intensity of the struggle and the strength of the joy that goes with it. Whatever is happening, these performers are not becoming less human, less distinctive. In the fullness of their skill and their joy, another is made present. So with Jesus; this is a human life and a human will whose power and joy is the performance of who God is and what God wants, the performance of the Word of God. When the early Christians insisted that we could not imagine sin in Jesus, they were not saying something negative but something positive; there is nothing in this performance that blocks out the composer. And when they insisted that there was no 'gap' in Jesus' humanity where God fitted in, they were insisting that this was the performance of one work only – the humanity of the performer is most full and real *in* the performance. We wouldn't be very impressed if, in the middle of some great performance, the singer or player stopped and said, 'Let me tell you how *I* feel about this, what I'd like to say.'

There is one agent, then, one living reality, God's word existing eternally in power and playing itself out in translated form in the human being, Jesus. Two 'sorts' of life, but in practice lived in one flow of action. The Creed tells us that Jesus' life on earth begins by the action of the Holy Spirit and through the Virgin Mary, and this is meant to unpack a little what is being thought about. We haven't of course, heard about the Holy Spirit yet in the Creed, though there will be more to say about this third dimension of God later on; this is just a sort of 'taster' for the later sections, where we shall have to think more carefully about that aspect of God's life that bridges heaven and earth, that makes the eternal Son alive within creation. When the Creed says that these two ways of looking at Jesus' birth, through the Spirit and through Mary, both need to be affirmed, it says that we can't think of the life of Jesus as just the result of what human history throws up, another episode in the world. God's action underpinning and animating the world must be particularly near the surface here. Yet it is also human history that opens the way.

Jesus comes into being on earth because God breathes into the world his 'breath' (which is what 'Spirit' of course means) – as he breathed into the first human being in the creation story of Genesis. But this doesn't happen without the human event of Mary saying 'yes'. I suggested earlier on some reasons for not just writing off the doctrine of Jesus being born of a virgin; but the really significant point is that human consent, human openness to God's inbreathing, is part of the moment. God doesn't override history, sweep it aside and produce a specially created something-or-other in the world; God invites the consent of a person who will nurture Jesus physically and spiritually into becoming the perfect vehicle of God that he has the capacity to be.

Somehow the whole history of God's ancient people comes into focus here, the history of a people who have received grace and gifts from God and who have had to 'take responsibility' for God in the world. All that God has given to his chosen community is gathered to a point as Mary is asked if she will take responsibility in a unique way for God in the world; she is asked to breathe in the breathing of God and to nurture God's embodiment in her body and in her commitment of emotion and thought and care. Jesus begins to be as a human being because of this meeting of God's free grace and Mary's grace-filled human readiness and openness.

Only three human individuals are mentioned in the Creed, Jesus, Mary and Pontius Pilate: that is Jesus; the one who says 'yes' to him; and the one who says 'no' to him. You could say that those three names map out the territory in which we all live. Through our lives, we swing towards one pole or the other, towards a deeper 'yes' or towards a deeper 'no'. And in the middle of it all stands the one who makes sense of it all. Jesus – the one into whose life we must all try to grow, who can work with our 'yes' and can even overcome our 'no'.

And when we think about Mary, we should not be afraid of recognizing her special role. Sadly, she's been the focus of a lot of controversy over the centuries. Sometimes her importance has been bizarrely exaggerated, so that others have overreacted and tried to make little of her. At the very least, she is the first person to put her trust in the God who is shown in Jesus. She is at least our elder sister as a believer. And older sisters often have a rather distinctive role in helping younger siblings to grow up and discover things. An older sister who knows her business can make a great deal of difference.

Jesus, Mary and Pontius Pilate . . . those three names map out the territory in which we all live.

Mary knows her business. By her consent she makes Jesus possible in that place, at that time. And we should not be ashamed of looking to her to hold our hands from time to time as we take the first steps that may make Jesus possible in this time, in this place. It's quite hard to imagine the depth and the level and the cost of what is asked of her by God in Luke's story of the Annunciation; to look at her and meditate on her 'yes' and seek her friendship in prayer is not at all an eccentric or foolish thing for a Christian to do if we want to grow in trust.

Around and beyond all these themes there is still the question, 'Why exactly is this life, Jesus' life, *required*? – What exactly is it about God's will and purpose that makes it necessary?' You could say that the 'incarnation' (literally, the 'en-fleshing'), the coming of the Son of God to this world in flesh and blood, is a natural outgrowth of how creation's whole story is developing; some

Christian thinkers have come close to saying that. But most of them, following what seems to be the more natural reading of the Bible, have wanted to say that it has something to do with what we as human beings *need*. It is from one point of view a way of dealing with a crisis or a brick wall in human affairs. Sometimes accounts of Christian teaching have concentrated first on this, and moved on to discuss the identity of Jesus and his relation to God; I've chosen to follow the way that the creeds deal with it, starting with the 'who' rather than the 'why'. Neither way is exclusively right; but it may help some people to see how what we say about Jesus builds on the whole pattern of *establishing that God is to be trusted*, before we examine in more depth just what the difference is that Jesus makes and why it needed making. If we can start from the conviction that the one who is speaking to us in the life of Jesus is to be relied upon, because he displays the self-consistency of God's love available and unbroken in all things, we may be more ready to trust what is being claimed as the result of this life – and death. If, in St Paul's words from the Letter to the Colossians, 'all the fullness of the Godhead dwells bodily' in Jesus, the recognition of this will help us see better how the act of God can be traced in Jesus and what it aims at.

DAVID JONES A Man for All Seasons,
Sanctus Christus de Capel-y-ffin (detail)

David Jones The Royal Banners, *Vexilla Regis* (1948)

FOUR

The Peace Dividend

He suffered and was buried,
and the third day he rose again

Peace and praise, reconciliation and delight; these are the purposes of God. But they are not at all in evidence in our world. Human lives are not in general very obviously reconciled to each other; the praise of God has to be listened for very hard. Across the ages, the image of God in the hearts and minds of human beings has too often been one that seems negative, frightening, trivial or all of these. The world is not where it might be, and where – if all we have been thinking about so far is true – it should be. God has made us and given us liberty to reflect his life, yet we use our minds and our freedom to protect ourselves rather than to pass on the life we have received. In St Luke's Gospel we read the story of the runaway son, the 'prodigal'; and when Jesus describes what the runaway's life was like when things went wrong, he says, in the stark words of the King James version of the Bible, 'no man gave unto him.' The familiar world is one in which people do not habitually give to each other as they could, let alone giving to God. It is a world with powerful defences between individuals, nations, ethnic groups, classes and religions.

So we're not where we could and should be, in a state where peace is sealed by what some like to call an 'economy of gift', living by one another's generosity. Day by day, in the most ordinary things of life, we acknowledge how basic such an economy is, just by the exchanges of family affection and routine courtesy or kindness; yet in our own lives and even more in the lives of the great collective realities in which we live, of nations and cultures, it constantly goes askew. And each of us knows how readily we will take the path of least resistance if giving to another becomes complicated or demanding or puts us at a real disadvantage. Pause between the last sentence and the next, as I do in writing this, and think of the last twenty-four hours . . . And the Christian belief that is summed up in the language of 'original sin' is basically a way of saying that this is a tangle that goes back to the very roots of humanity. The image that comes to mind is one familiar from the country roads of Monmouthshire in the days when, as Bishop of Monmouth, I travelled them each week to outlying parishes: miss one obscure sign, take one wrong turning, and you can't set it right just by another simple right turn. In humanity's history, the ingrained habit of turning inwards, turning in upon ourselves, is passed on. We learn how to be human only as we also learn the habits of self-absorption. We learn what we want, as some contemporary thinkers have stressed, by watching someone else wanting it and competing with them for it.

Before we begin to make choices, our options have been silently reduced in this way. To speak of original sin isn't necessarily to speak as if there were a great metaphysical curse hanging over the human race; it's just to observe that our learning how to exist is mixed in with learning what does *not* make for our life or our joy. And every failure and wrong turn in the history of a person as in the history of our species locks us more and more firmly into ourselves. No wonder we drift further and further from peace, become less and less free to give.

Something needs to reverse the flow, to break the cycle. Fearlessness in giving has to find its place at the heart of things, within the world of human exchange and interaction. It is only a tangible historical act, a human act that can break through all this; yet human beings, caught up in the cycle of rejection and defence, are not human enough to perform it. So we begin to see the outline of an answer to the question about why the life, the identity, of Jesus is needed. Only a human word, a human act will heal the process of human history; it isn't ideas and ideals that will do this, but some moment in history when relations are changed for good and all, when new things concretely become possible. But only the divine freedom is adequate to bring this about – because God's freedom (if you think back to the first chapter) has no trace of self-interest or self-defence. If we know what it means to trust the God who made the world, we can see where we must look for the action that will transform it.

Thus the apparently abstract language about Jesus as fully human and fully divine is rooted in this simple concern to find a human act that brings divine freedom into play in our world. Jesus is the human event that reverses the flow of human self-absorption because it is unconditionally open to the divine freedom.

Jesus' humanity is soaked through with the divine response to God the Father – it is a life that embodies God the Son or God the Word; and so it is a life without restriction, without rivalry or envy in its capacity for giving. At peace with God the Father, it is a life that makes peace in the human world wherever it is at work.

And that's it, surely, we might say; that's what we need to know. Jesus is perfect love made flesh and blood. Only it isn't quite so easy. In a world of blocked choices, wrong turnings and drastically false accounts of who and what we are, love of this sort is not going to look obvious or natural. It will seem to be against the grain. Worse still, the person who is free to give comes to be seen as an outsider, an enemy. In William Golding's chilling *Lord of the Flies*, Simon, the one child who has discovered that there is nothing for the other castaway boys to be afraid of, bursts into the circle of their improvised ritual dance (meant to placate the evil forces they dread) to tell them it's all right. And they turn on him and kill him.

The only fully human person is seen as the enemy of humanity. Once again, we don't have to look for complex and mystical theories to understand this; we have only to pause and recall the ways in which we find goodness unsettling, suspect – even the relief we feel if an exemplary person turns out not to be quite so good after all. Faced with real goodness, our instinct is often to run for cover. And this becomes even more marked when we look at patterns of 'scapegoating' in our social life: we reinforce our sense of belonging together by the arbitrary identifying of someone as an enemy or threat. And when someone tries to bridge the gaps thus set up and to make peace, we see deeper violence being drawn out. Within fairly recent history, the struggle for civil rights in the USA produced staggering levels of murderous violence against activists for racial justice – even, and especially, activists committed to non-violent methods. The murder of Martin Luther King in 1968 brought this to a shocking climax. If anyone takes on the responsibility for making peace they take on the risk of drawing out a violent 'no'; so that to take responsibility for God's credibility in the world, in the way we were thinking about earlier, is charged with risk. The more fully anyone takes this responsibility, the greater the risk.

Faced with real goodness, our instinct is often to run for cover.

If we speak of Jesus as a human being offering a divine gift, offering unrestricted love to the Father and to the world, we are speaking, necessarily, of someone who is going to be intensely and terribly unsafe in the world. He will be facing the weight of our inherited resistance; he will carry the cost of our ingrained revolt against who we really are. Christians talk of Jesus as 'paying the price of sin'. Sin, the state of revolt against truth, has consequences; it exacts a cost from us. If we live in untruth, in self-deceit, we are automatically condemned to undermining and destroying the life that is in us. We can't live against the grain of reality and expect to survive indefinitely (which is why our environmental crisis is such a powerful and poignant symbol of our corporate sinfulness). So when Jesus faces the final, uncompromising, violent rejection of the religious and political powers of his day, we can say that he 'embodies' not only the purposes and possibilities of God but the effects of the self-destructiveness of human beings.

The cost of human destructiveness: refugees fleeing Basra

Jesus, hanging on the cross, says to us, 'This is what your untruth means: you have been offered unconditional mercy and you turn from it in loathing. You have come to a place where you cannot recognize life itself for what it is. You don't know the difference between life and death. The reality in you is dead.' What is happening to Jesus – his dreadful physical suffering, his mental and spiritual torment as he cries to God asking why he has been forsaken – is a sort of picture of our ultimate fate, the death that is unreality, being cut off from what is true. In rejecting what Jesus has to give, we show where we are heading. In that sense, at least, he is carrying the burden of our sin – bearing the results of what we habitually do. St Paul says that he 'becomes' sin – that he becomes a sort of embodied image for what we are; and that he takes on himself the curse that is laid on us (2 Corinthians 5.21 and Galatians 3.13).

The New Testament reaches in several directions for words and images to make better sense of this. One of the most obvious and immediate is, of course, *sacrifice*. Sacrifice is, in Hebrew Scripture, the gift that makes peace with God. When you are alienated from God because of moral or ritual irregularity, you have to ask what you need to give in order to restore relationship – recognizing that the giving will be costly. And so it becomes possible to speak of Jesus as a sacrifice, Jesus paying to God the price of all that he is and does, so as to restore peace with the world. The Jewish thinkers of the immediate pre-Christian period had already formulated the idea, based on a good many passages in the Hebrew Scriptures, that a life of obedience was a kind of sacrifice, perhaps the only one that really mattered. Jesus' perfect harmony with God's purpose could obviously be seen as a sacrifice in that sense. But it was a harmony that led him to his death; obedience is a sort of blood sacrifice in this case. His blood is shed, like that of the sacrificial animals under the Law of Moses, so that there may be a clearing and restoration of communication between God and the world.

But there are other images. Jesus' death is a ransom, paid to our kidnappers (the powers of destruction); it is a punishment that we deserve, voluntarily borne by another, who is innocent; it is even a triumphant nailing up of a cancelled invoice. It's important to be aware of all these images and to try and see why they are used; equally important, though, not to treat them as if they were theories that explained why Jesus died. The single central thing is the conviction that for us to be at peace Jesus' life has to be given up. It isn't that a vengeful and inflexible God demands satisfaction, more that the way the world is makes it unavoidable that the way to our freedom lies through the self-giving of Jesus, even to the point of death. In the kind of world that you and I inhabit, the kind of world that you and I make or collude with, this is what the price of unrestricted love looks like. Hang on to that, and the jostling images and theories are kept in perspective. Appropriately, the Nicene Creed keeps it simple – just a few words: 'for us and for our salvation'. The everlasting Word of God begins a human life in the womb of Mary *for our sake*; and that 'for our sake' tells us how we are to read the whole story of Jesus. Many will remember the words of the children's hymn, 'There is a green hill far away'; elementary as they are, they contain the essentials:

> But we believe it was for us
> He hung and suffered there.

Just as simple and memorable is a phrase in the Eastern Orthodox liturgy, addressed to Christ: 'you left nothing undone until you had brought us to heaven.' Our theories about all this are likely to be convoluted and unsatisfactory; but all we need to know is that whatever it took – and takes – for us to be set free from our destructive and deceitful traps *has been done* through what happened on Good Friday. Jesus has plumbed the depths of human experience, including the terrible sense of abandonment by God that he endured on the cross; he has maintained his own peace with the Father throughout it, even in the heart of the protest wrung from him as he cries, 'Why?' He has travelled to the outermost limit of what our sin and untruthfulness produce – to the edges of hell.

'You left nothing undone until you had brought us to heaven.'

Some – like the great Reformer John Calvin and the modern Roman Catholic writer Hans Urs von Balthasar – have gone so far as to say that Jesus on the cross is enduring hell itself, the experience of final alienation from God. This is a difficult speculation, hard to state with consistency, but at least it reminds us how serious the cross is as a sign of God's willingness to accompany us through all the consequences of sin and finally to bring us back from the furthest point of distance from him that we could imagine. But when the Apostles' Creed says of Jesus that 'he descended into hell', the original meaning was not quite this. The Latin word simply meant 'the places beneath' and referred to a passage in the Letter to the Ephesians about Jesus descending to the lowest parts of creation as well as ascending to the heights, 'so that he might fill all things' (Ephesians 4.10). He goes, therefore, to those underground prisons where, in the thinking of some Jewish writers of Jesus' age, the spirits of those who had died resided. A similar idea appears in the First Letter of Peter (1 Peter 3.18–19), though there are several theories about what exactly is meant in this passage. It has been taken to mean that all those who had died before Christ's coming have the chance to hear the good news and to be transformed by it. This is the origin of the way in which Eastern Christians have long depicted the resurrection – not as Jesus rising from the grave but as Jesus breaking down the doors of a prison in which Adam and Eve, David and Solomon and other Old Testament characters are bound.

Once again, the theme is the open door that exists in the heart of every situation because of God's freedom. Even for those who didn't have the opportunity of literally meeting Jesus, the work of God in Jesus can be real; there is a way to peace and praise from any imaginable place, even the prison in which the dead live. Jesus has 'filled all things'; he is there in every human experience, opening the door. And so every place has changed.

When the Cold War ended, there was a great deal of talk about the 'peace dividend' – how, since we no longer needed so much money spent on nuclear weapons to defend ourselves against other people's nuclear weapons, there would be quantities of money available to spend on development and hunger and poverty and so on. As far as the world situation goes, we're still waiting. But it's a good metaphor for what's going on around the death of Jesus (and a metaphor that might make us more active and more impatient to see the literal peace dividend realized in our world). When peace is made, it's not just signing off on something; new possibilities are created, and energy is released for new things.

Which is why, when Christians talk of salvation, they don't *just* mean the crucifixion (though it may sound that way very often); they have in mind the whole series of events around Good Friday and Easter, the cross and the resurrection. Out of this series of events comes the new world, the new creation that St Paul speaks about. The crucifixion of Jesus, we could say, clears the ground, establishes God's presence in the middle of the worst of our world. But then there is a building, a realizing of possibilities. If we now know that all the weight of the hellish alienation we invite for ourselves is not enough to crush the eternal love of God, our eyes are open to see and grasp how that love remakes us.

The resurrection is in part about the sheer toughness and persistence of God's love. When we have done our worst, God remains God – and remains committed to being our God. God was God even while God in human flesh was dying in anguish on the cross; God is God now in the new life of Jesus raised from death. But what is interesting about the stories of the resurrection as we read them in the Bible is that they are not a series of general statements as to how the love of God is more powerful than evil or sin. They say that just as people met God's absolute love in the face and presence, the physical presence, of Jesus of Nazareth, so they still do. They hear the call of God and encounter the mercy of God in the same face and form of Jesus – who, in the resurrection stories, does what he always did, calling the disciples to him, breaking bread with them, teaching them what the Scriptures say. The resurrection displays God's triumphant love as still and for ever having the shape of Jesus. And this is why it won't do to reduce the resurrection just to something that was going on inside the heads of the disciples. If

When we have done our worst, God remains God.

we go down that road, we lose sight of the conviction that seems so basic in the Bible, that the disciples meet a risen Jesus who is still doing what he always did, making God present in his actual presence, his voice and touch. I don't see how we can say all that without taking completely seriously what the New Testament says about the tomb being empty on Easter Day.

But something is added. According to John's Gospel, he 'breathes into' his disciples his 'spirit', the breath of his life, so that they become equipped to do what he does and to speak with his voice to God and to the world. By breathing into the disciples, he sets up a chain of human contact coming down to our own day, a chain of voices and faces in which Jesus is active. The personal and direct contact with Jesus that is there before the crucifixion is renewed in the resurrection; and it is then taken to a new level as Jesus equips his friends to take responsibility for him and his Father, to be his body in the world. It is the great new metaphor of the New Testament. Contact with human beings who have received the breath of Jesus' life is contact with Jesus, as specific human beings pass on the mystery of God to each other across the ages. To meet a Christian in whom this spirit is working is to be contemporary with Jesus.

Remember, Christianity is a contact before it is a message. God is at work, God is communicating himself in flesh and blood, from the first moment Mary embraces her child. God is at work in this presence even when Jesus is saying nothing particular and doing nothing particular. And now God is at work in the continuing fellowship of flesh and blood human beings who have received Jesus' breath in themselves – even at the (frequent) moments when they are not doing anything specifically Christlike, there is something to be touched and sensed in the sheer thereness of the Christian community. If the risen Jesus is not an idea or an image but a living person, we meet him in the persons he has touched, the persons who, whatever their individual failings and fears, have been equipped to take responsibility for his tangible presence in the world.

Because Jesus as an individual is no longer an inhabitant of this world. 'He ascended into heaven' say the creeds, recalling the stories in Luke's Gospel and the Acts of the Apostles about how Jesus says goodbye to the disciples and is carried into heaven. This is pictorial language, of course, not to be interpreted as if the Bible were thinking of a sort of space travel. The biblical writers knew quite well that God did not live in a literal place above the clouds, but they happily used the strong images of Old Testament poems and psalms to tell us that after a while Jesus appeared no more in material form to his disciples. He 'ascended', he left the scene, and he now 'is seated at the right hand of the Father': when we look at God, we can't help but see Jesus. What he is, says and does is now forever and inseparably merged with what God is; he is part of our sense and understanding of the divine life. Going back to our main theme, Jesus has shown at a new level what it means for God to be trustworthy by showing him at work in every human situation; and the trustworthiness of God as creator, his selfless attention to what is other than himself, is made concrete in Jesus.

Father and Son, so to speak, witness to each other's faithfulness and credibility.

And this 'witness' to each other, this pointing to each other, is what is communicated in the 'breath of Jesus' life', in the mysterious agency we call the Holy Spirit – literally, of course, the Holy Breath. What holds together the community of Jesus' friends is this breathing the same air, being enlivened by the same spirit, so that all who are called into relation with Jesus are at the same time given the capacity to relate to God the Father as Jesus did. According to John's Gospel, Jesus says to Mary Magdalene, when he appears to her on Easter Day, that he is 'ascending to my Father *and your Father*'. Paul is talking about the same thing when he says that the Spirit makes it possible for Christians to say 'Abba, Father' to God – using the same Aramaic word Jesus used in his prayers. So to receive, to breathe in the breath of God is to receive the intimacy Jesus has with God, the unashamed boldness in coming into God's presence that is the right thing for a real member of the family to feel. Every time we say, 'Our Father who art in Heaven', we're making a big statement about what we believe; we're saying that Jesus is now the atmosphere we live in. In him, in the strength of his holy breath, we grow up into intimacy with God, trustful and natural and deeply demanding all at once.

The atmosphere has changed; the world has changed. No wonder Paul speaks about a 'new creation' coming into existence when we breathe the breath of Jesus. Some of the poets of the Church have spoken of Easter Day as a sort of 'extra' day of creation, an eighth day of the week: the seven days of the first creation are all taken up and taken forward in a new history of the world, where everything begins again. St John in his Gospel very gently reminds us that Jesus' tomb was in a garden – like the Garden of Eden; and Mary Magdalene, when she first sees the risen Jesus, thinks he is the gardener.

When we celebrate Easter, we are really standing in the middle of a second 'Big Bang', a tumultuous surge of divine energy as fiery and intense as the very beginning of the universe. What a recent writer wonderfully calls 'the fire in the equations,'[9] the energy in the mathematical and physical structures of things, is here at Easter; and when in the ancient ceremonies of the night before Easter we light a bonfire and bless it and light candles from it, we may well think of the first words of God in Genesis, 'Let there be light!' On Easter Eve, we begin the readings with the story of creation itself, because that's what we are now witnessing, the creative power re-establishing the whole world.

When we celebrate Easter, we are really standing in the middle of a second 'Big Bang'.

The Easter liturgy is heady stuff, and we may well need a bit of a reality check in case we find ourselves imagining that the history of the world as we know it is over. The New Testament certainly suggests that some early Christians were so overwhelmed by all this that they spoke as if the final resurrection of the dead had already happened and the end of the world had

Easter at Agio Thomas, Athens, as people leave the church with their candles

come (St Paul has to put them straight in a couple of places). The truth is that, while at one level, we and the whole of creation have 'passed from death to life', the history of the world is still going on and is still all too visibly a history of rebellion and suffering. Does it *look* as if the world has been renewed and redeemed? Not often.

The reality of the new creation is that every moment of our history has now been opened to a future of healing and promise; but from moment to moment the possibility and the reality remain of struggle, uncertainty. The future is just that – the future: not something we can know and control. It is in God's hands, ultimately, and we have been given the confidence that God is the end of the story and that our history cannot just fall away into final, irredeemable chaos. Scholars of the New Testament have been talking for generations about the tension in the Bible between the already and the not yet. The New Testament writers clearly think there is something to hope for, but they stress that hope is by its nature something projected into the dark ('Who hopes for what they can see already?' asks Paul in the Letter to the Romans 8.25).

So at this point in the Creeds we are reminded of the 'not yet': Christ is going to 'come again in glory to judge the living and the dead'. And until that last trial, that last crisis (and 'crisis' is the Greek for 'judgement'), trials and crises can be expected. On the far side of all the testing, the pain and struggle of our history, there is Jesus. Finally, beyond all our history, he will be there to try and test all things by his absolute truth; in his presence everything and everyone will finally be shown for what they are and find their true place.

But it is one thing to say that on the far side of every future is the light of Christ, which shows what the world truly is; it is another thing to get caught up in trying to work out the date of the Second Coming and the Last Judgement. This is quite a cottage industry among certain sorts of Christians. Yet what the New Testament actually says, again and again, is that we do not and cannot know the date of the final end, and that therefore we should live our lives as if the end might be at any moment – and at the same time, live our lives with complete responsibility for the here and now. St Paul is scathing about people who have given up their jobs because the end of the world is just round the corner (see 2 Thessalonians 3.6–12). Jesus himself is remembered as saying that even he, speaking as a human being, cannot give a date. And he simply tells us to keep awake, because we cannot know when he will come.

All we need to know about the Last Judgement is that it will happen and that we don't know when. So we have to live in a state of constant preparedness to encounter complete truth. Whether it happens tomorrow or in three million years makes absolutely no difference to what we should do next. We must learn to live now, immediately, in the light of Christ's truth. We can never use the Last Judgement as an alibi for not doing what is good in itself – caring for each other, making peace, above all, caring for our environment. It is one of the silliest and most unchristian things imaginable to say that we should not care for our material environment because it will be destroyed soon; that is exactly like the people Paul is so cross about who refuse to work because the end is nigh. It may flatter our vanity or our sense of drama to think that we have a clue about when the end will come. But it sounds very odd indeed in the light of the way the New Testament talks about it. Martin Luther apparently said that if he knew the world would end tomorrow, he would plant a tree – meaning that what is good today is just *good*: and it doesn't become somehow unimportant because the time frame is short. The difficult thing is getting a balance. St Paul reminds us that we need to do what is required of us here and now; but he also

> *So we have to live in a state of constant preparedness to encounter complete truth.*

reminds us that if we live in the light of the imminent coming of Christ, we need a profound detachment from the pressures of the here and now; we need a sense of what does matter and what doesn't in our lives and a freedom from loading all our expectations on the success of our projects and the degree of comfort and stability we can attain. We take our responsibilities with deep seriousness; and then we must learn to say, 'If we don't succeed in the way we wanted, so be it; God is still God.'

St John's Gospel more than any other bit of the Bible puts the stress on the here and now, on living 'in the light' – getting used to the terrifying questions that the truth of Jesus will put to us, to the way in which he exposes our excuses and self-deceptions. Christians pray daily in the Lord's Prayer, 'Lead us not into temptation' – a phrase that has puzzled many. But its original meaning is clear enough. We are to ask God not to bring us to trial – that is, not to bring us to face a crisis we're not prepared for. Don't bring us naked, fearful, helpless and confused into the presence of absolute truth and love; give us time to get used to the fierce light of Christ. Give us the bread we need for today's journey so that we may learn what is good today and be that bit more ready for tomorrow's testing – and for that ultimate testing of our honesty and truthfulness that is Christ's coming.

The New Testament constantly interweaves the two themes of the coming of Christ, the light, transparency, glory of his coming, and the daily task of putting to death our selfish and fearful habits. We have to live in the light of the end – not gloomily and fearfully, but trying to bring ourselves relentlessly out of the shadows where we hide from God and ourselves and each other. And when we read the Bible and celebrate the sacraments, what we are doing is repeatedly coming out of the shadows, back to where truth lives, where Jesus lives.

And that's worth underlining in this context, because it takes us back to where we started in this chapter. We don't learn the truth as isolated individuals, any more than we grow and discover as isolated individuals. The purpose of Jesus' ministry and death and resurrection is to re-create the community of God's people, and the peace that he makes between God and us is a peace that is also made with other human beings and with the creation of which we're part. We so easily make the mistake of thinking that peace or salvation is first a matter for each one of us alone; whereas the Bible always seems to take it for granted that we receive God's peace and mercy as part of the community that is created by God's word and action. So getting used to the light of truth is something that we do together as believers.

We don't learn the truth as isolated individuals.

The Holy Spirit, the breath of Jesus' life, is described in the Bible both as the Spirit that gives 'communion' and as the Spirit of truth – as if experiencing the truth that the Spirit conveys is always part of living the common life of Christ's 'Body', the assembly of God's people. The familiar prayer usually called the 'Grace' (taken from the end of Paul's Second Letter to the Corinthians) speaks of 'the grace of our Lord Jesus Christ, the love of God and the fellow-ship of the Holy Spirit'. 'Fellowship' is sometimes translated 'communion', and both these words represent *koinonia* in the Greek – a word much beloved of theologians these days, but in fact meaning simply 'sharing'. This isn't only 'sharing' in the sense of me sharing something with you by giving you something, but, more profoundly, sharing in the sense of having something in common, belonging to the same species or family or group, sharing a family resemblance. Perhaps from time to time we could do with a simplified version of the Grace that spoke of the free kindness of Jesus our Master and the shared life of his holy breath.

But this means that the life that happens when we breathe the air of God is always life *together*. Jesus remakes the people of God, the community of God's choosing, and he does it, not simply by binding lots of individuals to himself and then introducing them to each other (though there are elements of that, as we'll see); he transforms the whole structure and energy of a shared life – in the language of early Christian theology he transfigures the whole of our *nature*, what makes us human, what we have in common as people. Into our common 'nature' Jesus infuses something new and radical so deeply that it becomes the lifeblood of the community that acknowledges him. In the Old Testament, the people of Israel are bound together in the vision of justice, the absolute shared obligation to see God's righteousness worked out in every human situation, combined with the conviction that each and every Israelite is equally called by God. And in that deepened and enlarged community of which the New Testament speaks, its members are held together not only by justice and the common sense of calling, but by a pattern of mutual giving and mutual nourishment and mutual dependence. The human nature that we have in common in this new creation is a nature always in movement from one to the other and back again, bestowing life on each other (a pattern reflecting that of God the Father, the Son and the Holy Spirit, of course). So it *is* sharing as giving – but a giving that has become constitutive of what we are, part of the very definition of what we are as renewed human beings.

So, as we move forwards in this exploration, we shall have to think more about what it means for us to be always meeting God in company, in 'communion'. The most important thing about the peace dividend, the life that is made possible as the result of Christ's death and resurrection, is that it is *not* a peace that is just the absence of rivalry and conflict; it is an active condition of loving and nurturing, giving and receiving, mutuality. This is the newest and the deepest thing about the new world that Easter has brought to birth.

David Jones The Royal Banners, *Vexilla Regis*
(detail)

David Jones The Farm Door (1937)

FIVE

God in Company

And I believe one catholic and apostolic Church

Breathing the air of Christ, Christ becoming the 'atmosphere' in which we live – to borrow the language of a great New Testament scholar, C. F. D. Moule – isn't only about being in a *state* of peace but about being in what some would call a 'dynamic equilibrium'. Our peace is what it is because it is a flow of unbroken activity, the constant maintenance of relation and growth as we give into each others' lives and receive from each other, so that we advance in trust and confidence with one another and God. So it is that when the Creed moves us on to speak about believing in the Holy Spirit, it also moves us on to speak about our confidence, our trust in the Church.

For some, this feels awkward. Surely we don't 'believe in' the Church in the sense that we believe in God or in Christ? It's a fair point; and in fact it's already there in the original Greek of the Nicene Creed, which says literally that we *believe the Church*. The Church is indeed not another reality on the same level as the Father, the Son and the Spirit. But it is a community we can trust.

Just as we can trust God because he has no agenda that is not for our good, so we can trust the Church because it is the sort of community it is, a community of active peacemaking and peacekeeping where no one exists in isolation or grows up in isolation or suffers in isolation. The slogan of the Church's life is 'not without the other'; no I without a you, no I without a we. Yet that doesn't mean that the identity of the Church is a 'herd' identity, with everyone's individuality submerged in the collective. The difference between I and you remains real difference – otherwise there would be no challenge about it. You may have noticed that few churches are characterized by drab sameness; when people try to create a herd mentality in the Church, whether in a local congregation or in a wider institution, it tends to break down dramatically, sooner or later.

So believing in the Church is really believing in the unique gift of the *other* that God has given you to live with. The New Testament sees the Church as a community in which each person has a gift that only they can give into the common life. We Christians are so used to the imagery the Bible uses, especially the great metaphor of Christ's 'Body', that we forget just how radical and comprehensive is the vision of a community of universal giftedness. The ancient world had sometimes used the image of the body to describe a society in which there were different *functions*, a very natural use for such language. But it was left to Christians to reconceive this in terms of different gifts, and to draw out the further revolutionary implication, that the frustration of any one member is the frustration of all – because then there is something that is not being properly given. Someone has not been granted the freedom to offer what only they can give to the whole.

When St Paul speaks about the Church as the Body of Christ, especially in his letters to Christians in Rome and Corinth, this is what is at the forefront of his mind. The Church is a diverse community, but its diversity is not just a natural diversity of temperaments or preferences – we trivialize the idea if that's all there is to it. It has a diversity of gifts given by the Spirit, a diversity of relationships with God, we might say, out of which come diverse perspectives on God and diverse ways of making God's work real for each other.

And this is an intensely practical and moral principle – indeed you could rightly say that for St Paul this was where all Christian morality started. Look, for example, at the Second Letter to the Corinthians (chapters 8 and 9), where Paul is writing about the question of the relative wealth and poverty of different churches. Some have more than they need; others don't have enough. This means that some are being frustrated in what they are free to give. So Paul says to the wealthier churches, 'Equip them from what you don't need; and who knows? They may be able to give to you in due course.' It's a very basic and simple application of a principle that permeates the whole of Paul's vision. If you have a gift, it's there so that you can help another to become a giver in turn. God's gift makes givers. But notice too how the converse works: later in the same letter, Paul speaks about his own experience of being made to suffer when other Christians are made to suffer. 'Who is weak and I am not weak?' he asks. When another Christian is frustrated, held back from growing, Paul too is held back. We grow only together.

It is, incidentally, a powerful indication of what is new and mysterious about the role of ministry in the Christian community. The apostle, the public witness of Jesus' resurrection, who directs the thoughts and prayers of the Church, is the one in whom the porous boundaries of life in Christ are most pronounced, the one who senses most acutely both the joy and the pain of other believers. The apostle's ministry is thus not essentially one of control but one of literal com-passion, suffering with, and con-gratulation, rejoicing with. That is something to ponder for those of us who hold 'apostolic' roles in the Church; it should not be like the priesthoods and hierarchies of ancient religion, because it is to do with inhabiting the common life with a particular intensity, so that the minister can point with authority to what is basic in this common life. Being a Christian priest or minister isn't about managing religious technology for an uninstructed public but about witnessing to the distinctive character of a common life in which each depends on all.

So a well-functioning Christian community is going to be one in which everyone is working steadily to release the gifts of others. And this is not for the sake of some abstract self-fulfilment: the Christian community is not a place where everyone is crying out, 'Get out of my way so that I can exercise *my* gift' (though the phenomenon is not unknown ...). In the context of the 'Body', the gift of each is inseparable from the need of each. The giver has to understand both how the gift is to be given into the common life, and has to be aware of what the common life and the obstinate reality of others must give for one's own life to be real and solid. What you could call the 'density' of relationships in the Church has to do with the *attention* that everyone is called to, attention to yourself, to each other and to the whole complex in which God is at work. Once we have grasped that the gift of each is unique, we have to learn equally that the need of each is unique, and is just as much to do with God.

A well-functioning Christian community is . . . one in which everyone is working steadily to release the gifts of others.

C. S. Lewis once famously described a 'charitable' person in these terms: 'She lived for others; you could tell the others by their hunted look.' We can think about our gifts as though they licensed us to impose what we had to give; we can think about our gifts as though we had nothing to receive; and we can think about our needs in dependent and immature ways. But the solid reality of a really functioning Christian community is like that of a good marriage, in which mutual attention, giving and receiving, enjoyment and sacrifice are tightly woven together, as both realize that there is nothing good for one that is not good for both, nothing bad for one that is not bad for both, that fullness of life is necessarily a collaborative thing.

Of course, the Bible suggests that this is the wrong way round – we get our sense of what makes a good marriage from our understanding of the Body of Christ. But concretely and practically, we all have some idea of how good marriages work and it may not be such a bad place to start. If we talk in the abstract about gifts and sacrifices in the life of the Church, there is always the suspicion that somebody else is defining for you what you have to sacrifice and not listening when you want to think about your gifts. Yet somehow in the specific context of a good marriage it becomes more intelligible. If I really have no interest that is *just* mine in a marriage, there may be circumstances where I have to question what I think I want, where I must hold back and think again about my aims. Equally, what matters to the other partner is that I am *I*, not some bloodless fantasy that suits them, so that what makes for my life and health matters to the other. What we believe about the Church is that this sort of close interweaving is the lifeblood of an entire community, extended without limit in time and space.

The good life is not simply one in which certain rules are kept.

I've said that this is the wellspring of St Paul's idea of morality. The good life is not simply one in which certain rules are kept – this is always at best a shorthand for the results of life together in the Body. The good life is one in which we have learned how to be for each other, and in so being to live fully as ourselves. If lying, killing, adultery, greed and so on are sinful, it is because we couldn't imagine a community, such as the Body of Christ is meant to be, in which things like this went unchallenged. As you will probably have noticed, the Church in human history is regularly a place where such patterns of behaviour can go unchallenged for a long time; you couldn't necessarily work out what the Church was meant to be from telling the Church's story. But as soon as the Church starts trying to explain why it's there in the first place, the logic of its existence, it's impossible not to be looking back to these fundamentals.

Church history or no Church history, we need moments when we can say, '*That's* what I mean by Church.' And so when we try to think through just what it is we're trusting or believing when we say we believe the Church, we need two things. First, we need a way of thinking about the Church that allows us to say that on certain particular occasions, when the Christian community is doing certain particular things, we know that this is what the Church *really* is, independent of our successes and failures, our efforts or our laziness. Second, we need to be able to tell stories of the *unexpected* points at which the Church 'comes through'. In addition to the regular, theologically defined moments when the Church is supposed to be 'just' the Church, it helps to have the fleshing out of this in specific bits of human experience. Just as, earlier on, we were noting how language about God only comes alive when we can tell stories of human lives in which we can see what 'God' actually means, so also with the Church.

In its original Latin the Apostles' Creed announces belief in the *communio sanctorum*; and this could mean one of two things – or maybe both. It could be 'the sharing between holy people' or it could mean 'the sharing of holy things'. Now when the New Testament, especially St Paul, talks about 'holy people', it doesn't mean quite what we might mean by 'saints', it isn't offering a sort of verdict on a lot of spectacularly good lives. Christian people are 'holy' simply because they have been adopted by God into relationship, into that family relationship expressed in saying 'Our Father'. So the 'sharing between holy people' isn't some kind of club for the spiritually gifted; it's simply the relationship that holds together those who recognize and express their adoption by God. And so this sharing becomes tangible and visible when Christians are together just breathing the air of Christ, making real in words and actions who they are in relation to Jesus. The 'communion' that is meant here is what becomes visible when Christians are simply saying who they are.

And what does this involve? The Church is the community of those who have been 'immersed' in Jesus' life, overwhelmed by it. Those who are baptized have disappeared under the surface of Christ's love and reappeared as different people. The waters close over their heads, and then, like the old world rising out of watery chaos in the first chapter of the Bible, out comes a new world. So when the Church baptizes people, it says what it is and what sort of life its people live. Baptism is an event in which the 'sharing between holy people' comes to light and we see what the Church really is, a community in which people are constantly being brought into new life by being given a new relationship with God and each other.

The Church is the community of those who have been 'immersed' in Jesus' life, overwhelmed by it.

It is also the community of those who are invited to eat with

The bread of life, broken for us

Jesus. Just as, in his earthly life, Jesus expressed his promise to create a new people of God by sharing meals with unlikely people, just as, after the resurrection, he shares food with his disciples as he re-calls them to their task, so it is with the whole Church. We are in the Church because we have been invited, not because we have earned our place. And so when the Church gathers to eat and drink with Jesus in Holy Communion, the Church once again says who and what it is. In baptism and Holy Communion, the nature of the Church is laid bare for us. What is the Church? Is it simply those who have been immersed in, soaked in the life of Jesus, and who have been invited to eat with him and pray to the Father with him.

These two events are rooted in what the New Testament tells us that Jesus told his friends to do. The night before his death, he tells them to repeat the meal of bread and wine because he will be with them in and through the eating and drinking. And after his resurrection, according to St Matthew, he tells the disciples to go and baptize the whole creation. That is why these two actions are regarded by most Christians as the most important ritual actions of the Church. Most Christians also regard other things as crucially meaningful actions, 'sacraments' that show what the Church is and renew it in its proper identity by God's grace – marriage, for example, and the recognition and commissioning of those called to lifelong public ministry. But after the Reformation those who called themselves Protestants argued that baptism and Holy Communion had to be on a different level from the others because they were commanded clearly in the Bible and dealt with the most basic facts about the Church.

Holy Communion certainly has been seen by practically all Christians as the essential unifying and identifying activity. In the New Testament, it is introduced to us as the 'covenant' meal, like the meals that in the Old Testament were associated with sacrifices that sealed the alliance between God and God's people. The sacrificial animal was slaughtered – a gift given to make peace between God and us – and then portions of the animal were shared out to celebrate the renewal or confirmation of God's promise to be with us, and the blood was sprinkled on the holy place. Jesus seems to be saying that after his death – the gift that once and for all makes peace – the meal we share is a receiving of the gift that has made peace, like the eating of the sacrificial bull or sheep. This food is the body and blood of the one sacrificed. And here the blood is not poured out on the altar or sprinkled on the people; it is consumed by the people – a very shocking image for Jews, who were forbidden to drink blood because it was the 'life principle' of any living being. Jesus is taking the covenant idea and pushing it further: *this* blood, *this* life is something we must take into our own lives, it is not something that renews us from outside.

When at the Last Supper Jesus speaks of his blood which is being shed on the day after as 'blood of the covenant', he is saying that the eating and drinking of bread and wine in memory of him is a renewal and confirmation of God's promise, like the Old Testament sacrificial meal – though it goes further and it is always a re-calling, a re-presenting, of the one event of Jesus' death, not a series of constantly repeated rituals (that is the main argument of the very difficult Letter to the Hebrews in the New Testament). Here is the most literal peace dividend of all, as we are guaranteed the effects of Christ's death through receiving his life into our own – in the physical signs of bread and wine and in the faith and trust that goes with this action.

Notoriously, this is an area where Christians have got themselves into great complications and bitter controversy. Anyone trying to make sense of Holy Communion today has to find a way through a minefield of complexities, or so it can seem. But there are things that everyone recognizes as basic, and one of them is this notion of covenant – the promise renewed and affirmed. Some of the great eighteenth-century Protestant hymn writers such as Isaac Watts and Philip Doddridge liked to speak of the bread and wine of Communion as 'pledges', 'sacred pledges'. A pledge is a sign of something promised, a secure testimony to what will be enjoyed later on; and that is at the very least what has to be said about the bread and wine: they are the visible signs of promise, foreshadowing the fellowship we shall enjoy through Jesus with the Father.

But the urge to say more than this has always been very strong; and of course it has a lot to do with those mysterious words spoken by Jesus at the Last Supper, 'This is my body; this is my blood.' Perhaps the place to begin in thinking about this is to hear it as Jesus saying of the bread, 'This *too* is my body; this is as much a carrier of my life and my identity as my literal flesh and blood.' We have all too easily got caught up in debates that sound as though they were about a sort of magical transposition of Jesus' literal flesh and the bread of Communion; but the force of the Gospel text (especially when read alongside the great meditation in the sixth chapter of John's Gospel on 'the bread that comes down from heaven') seems to be more to do with a kind of extension of the reality of Jesus' presence to the bread and wine. They too bear and communicate the life of Jesus, who and what he is. By eating these, the believer receives what the literal flesh and blood have within them, the radiant action and power of God the Son, the life that makes him who he is.

This 'extension', this inclusion of the bread and wine in Jesus' identity so that his presence is there in them, is not brought about by any kind of magic. Throughout a great deal of the history of Christian thinking about Holy Communion, it has been associated with the action of the Holy Spirit. Just as the Holy Spirit in the New Testament literally brings Jesus into the world in the conception of the child in Mary's womb, and just as the Spirit 'brings to birth' all those adopted by God and enables them to pray in the voice of Jesus, so the Spirit 'overshadows' the bread and wine and fills them with new life. It is a dimension of the sacrament specially under-lined in the thinking of Eastern Christians, who often rebuke Westerners for playing this down. For them, the great moment in the service is not just the recital of what happened at the Last Supper, but the prayer that follows, asking for the Spirit to change the bread and wine.

The pattern that slowly emerges is something like this. When we come together to pray at Holy Communion, we do so as baptized believers, people whose lives have been 'soaked' in the life of Jesus by the coming into our lives of the Spirit. And so our prayer is, so to speak, dropped into his, absorbed into his. We stand before God the Father, clothed in the identity of Jesus by the gift of the Spirit. We prayerfully give into Jesus' hands the bread and the wine, so that *his* prayer may be made over them. His prayer is that they should become his body and blood. What he prays for happens, because he is the perfect channel of the Holy Spirit's action. So the bread and wine are given back to us, transformed by the Spirit, to make us more deeply what we already are, to confirm the bond that God has created between himself and us.

The congregation assembled for the 'Eucharist', the Thanks-giving – to give it one of its oldest and most meaningful names – is standing in the midst of the fire, like the three young men in the fiery furnace in the Old Testament Book of Daniel (chapter 3); and, as in that strange and wonderful story the three young Jews who are being persecuted by the Babylonian king walk unharmed through the fire because a fourth figure, who is 'like a Son of God', walks with them, so we walk in the fire of God's love accompanied by the eternal Son of God, who has welcomed us into his company. To use yet another Old Testament image, from Exodus this time (chapter 24), we see God and we eat and drink, as the elders of Israel do on the top of the holy mountain after the covenant sacrifice has been offered. And more than one poet and preacher in the history of the Church has written of this in terms of the fire from heaven that falls on the offering of the prophet Elijah (1 Kings 18). Holy Communion is a real 'pentecostal' experience – like the great event at the beginning of the Church's story that is told by St Luke in Acts chapter 2, the fire coming down on the disciples as they gather in obedience to the risen Christ.

When we receive the bread and wine at Communion, we are nearest the very heart of what it is to be a Christian and to be the Church. We stand in the power of his prayer; we stand there because we have been invited by the risen Jesus, just as he invited sinners to eat with him in his life on earth; we pray in the Holy Spirit and we receive gifts that the Holy Spirit has made to be vehicles of this life. It is a moment when we declare who we are and when we are given the greatest opportunity to grow as believers because we are as open as we can be to the act of God in Jesus and the Spirit.

When we receive the bread and wine at Communion, we are nearest the very heart of what it is to be a Christian and to be the Church.

In the old Church of England Prayer Book, the Lord's Prayer is said after Holy

Communion – as if to remind us that when we have eaten and drunk our identity as God's adopted children is renewed. In the newer services and in the Roman Catholic tradition, it is said immediately *before* Communion, as if to say that we are never more fully our baptized and renewed selves than when we are coming to eat and drink at Jesus' table. Both traditions have a logic to them, and it is a logic that depends on the centrality of the Spirit's work in this event. We have the greatest right and justification to say 'Our Father' when the bread and wine are in our hands or our mouths. And it does us good to be reminded too of the introduction to the Lord's Prayer that has always been used in the Roman Catholic service at this point – we 'dare' to say 'Our Father', we have the nerve to say 'Our Father'. It is no automatic or prosaic thing; we have been given licence to say something miraculous and outrageous because of God's goodness.

So, here is the real Church, the Church doing nothing but being the Church, fully absorbed into Christ's prayer and adoration. No wonder that one of the ancient hymns about the Eucharist says that the end of the world has arrived:

> Alpha and Omega, to whom shall bow
> All nations at the Doom, is with us now.

What happens at this moment of Communion is a foretaste of where everything is heading – ourselves and the things of this world represented by the bread and wine all caught up in the action of the Spirit in an event of reconciliation and adoration, the reflection of God's goodness and glory. And, of course, if we are paying attention at Holy Communion, we shall learn that this showing forth of what the Church is gives us a clear standard by which we can judge ourselves as a Church. This is what God means the Church to be – a community gathered into one because it prays Jesus' prayer and is fed by his life and power; a community in which all are equal because everyone is equally an undeserving and surprising guest; and so a community that displays God's freedom in loving and forgiving, and is at peace with creation as well as Creator.

I've often preached – like others, I'm sure – on how, when we come back to our places after taking Communion, we ought to look at our next-door neighbours with awe and amazement. The person next to me – whom I may love deeply, may not know at all, may dislike, may even fear – is God's special, honoured guest, praying Christ's prayer, living from Christ's life. Just for this moment, they are touched with the glory of the end of all things; and so are we. And here are the things of the world, God's natural gifts, turned into effective signs of God's re-creation and renewing love. They too are what God wants them to be at the end of everything, signs of overflowing love.

The person next to me – whom I may love deeply, may not know at all, may dislike, may even fear – is God's special, honoured guest.

But there is another dimension to all this, which is of equal importance. When Christians meet for worship, they don't just share bread and wine; they gather to be told who they are, not only in action but in word, in story and song and above all in the story and song that is the Bible. The Church shows itself as what it truly is as it listens to the Bible. It is gathered so that it can listen to what is now its own story, not just the record of people long ago. The sharing of holy things in Holy Communion takes place in the context of listening to this story, the story of God's dealings with the world in which God shows who he is; and as that story is read and reflected on, the community recognizes that it belongs in the same frame of reference. It lives here and now in fellowship with all those that God has invited and inspired. In the Sunday congregation, Abraham, Moses, Ezekiel and the rest stand invisibly alongside us; we are part of a covenant people whose origins go right back to the invisible distance, barely known outside legend and epic, yet absolutely real and continuous. The life we now share, the sharing between holy people, is a life shared with those whom God called in the unimaginable past, in the obscure and shadowy history of Middle Eastern nomads in the Bronze Age and before.

This is why Christians say that the Bible is 'the Word of God' here and now. A word is spoken and heard; when the Bible is read to us in the midst of the congregation, it is God who is telling us our history and our identity. Martin Luther said of the Bible, *de te loquitur*, 'it's talking about you'. In that

Martin Luther said of the Bible . . . 'it's talking about you'.

sense, Scripture always stands alongside sacrament as the measure of who we are. The listening Church is the Church being what it is, just as the Church sharing bread and wine is the Church as it truly is.

It's worth taking a moment to clarify some of the misunderstandings that can arise for Christians about the Bible. It is, we often say, the Word of God; but it is the Word of God not because it is the primary and central witness in history to God – Jesus Christ is that – but because it is the primary witness to Jesus Christ. And when it is read in the community of believers, it is used by the Spirit to bring God's calling alive for us. In other words, it is not a sort of magical text, supernaturally giving us guaranteed information about everything under the sun. What we call its 'inspiration' is its capacity to be the vehicle of the Holy Spirit, making Jesus vividly present to our minds and hearts, and so making his challenge and invitation immediate for us.

Christians of the Protestant tradition have tended to think about the Bible as if it were first and foremost a book that people read in private. This is an understandable reaction to a situation in which individuals were not encouraged to read it in private and were entirely dependent on an elite of clerical experts to tell them about it. But it was a bit of an *over*-reaction, all the same. At the very beginning of the Church's life, it was definitely a book that was read in community – as the Old Testament was read in the synagogues. In those early Christian centuries, for one thing, very few people could afford a library of several dozen scrolls, hand-copied. We think of the Bible as a single book between covers, but this could only have been the case from relatively late in the Church's history. In the earliest days and through the early Middle Ages, the Bible was a collection of books read by and in communities, in the context of prayer and regular meditative interpretation. What went wrong in the later Middle Ages seems to have been that the Bible had been split up into tiny segments, texts that were used to prove points rather than to open up the history of God's work. There were exceptions (and St Thomas Aquinas had insisted strongly that what mattered most was the literal sense of the Bible and its narratives of people meeting God); the mystery plays of the period gave a selective but very powerful representation of the 'big picture'. But overall there had been a loss in understanding the significance of this; and also there was little sense that the Bible might have awkward questions to put to the Church in its present form.

Initially, the Reformation was an attempt to put the Bible at the heart of the Church again – not to give it into the hands of private readers. The Bible was to be seen as a public document, the charter of the Church's life; all believers should have access to it because all would need to know the common language of the Church and the standards by which the Church argued about theology and behaviour. The huge Bibles that were chained up in English churches in the sixteenth century were there as a sign of this. It was only as the rapid development of cheap printing advanced that the Bible as a single affordable volume came to be within everyone's reach as something for individuals to possess and study in private. The leaders of the Reformation would have been surprised to be associated with any move to encourage anyone and everyone to form their own conclusions about the Bible. For them, it was once again a text to be struggled with in the context of prayer and shared reflection.

Christians of the Reformed traditions have come to pride themselves on the way they have made the Bible accessible to everyone, and that is not wrong. But what badly needs to be recovered now is the sense that the Bible is to be read *in company*. It is not just a book that can be opened and read anywhere; it has a unique role in representing to the gathered group as it meets for worship the acts of God in making a people for himself. Private and individual reading follows on from that, and is informed by it. Even when I read the Bible on my own, I must remember that I read it in the company of readers across the ages – and I have to be ready to learn from them as from my contemporaries.

What badly needs to be recovered now is the sense that the Bible is to be read in company.

Incidentally, this throws a little light on some of the vexed questions about what the inspiration of the Bible implies. If the Bible is first and foremost a single book between covers – a modern book, essentially – and a book that is there for individuals to read, it is possible to get very agitated about whether it is completely reliable. Its inspiration has to be proved and defended in terms of its obvious correctness about every detail of history or science. If it is shown not to be accurate about this sort of thing, its whole credibility is affected. But if, on the other hand, it is a collection of texts consistently used by the Holy Spirit to renew and convert the

Melanesian Brothers read the Scriptures together

Church, something to which the Church constantly refers to test its own integrity as it meets and thinks together, the issue of whether it is all totally accurate by modern standards of history or science becomes less important. Genesis may not tell us how the world began in the way a modern cosmologist would; but it tells us what God wants us to know, that we are made by his love and freedom alone. The Book of Daniel may be at odds with what we know about Babylonian history; but it tells us what God wants us to know about the imperative of faithfulness in a tyrannical and ungodly empire. And while we are on a different kind of ground with – say – the Gospel stories, which were written down so close to the time of the events narrated, it is still true that contradictions of detail between different Gospels are not the end of the world; they tell us what God wants us to know. Did Jesus' driving of the moneychangers out of the Temple happen at the beginning or the end of his public career? John's Gospel says one thing, the other

Gospels say something different. But the force of the story is the same; *de te loquitur*, it's about you.

In all that I've said so far in this chapter, I've been trying to give some sense of what you could call the moral heart, the moral energy of the Church, an energy so like that of a working marriage; and trying to give some sense of why we need those moments of shared experience when we are told in word and sacrament who we are, and, just for a moment, really *are* what we're meant to be. The Nicene Creed sums a lot of this up by describing the Church as 'one, holy, catholic and apostolic'. It is one because God's call is one and the same, God's Son is one and the same, God's Spirit is one and the same. We're not one because we have managed to find a more or less satisfactory level of agreement among ourselves, but because there is one invitation to one relationship with God the Father. This unity is expressed always in very diverse ways, but it is not a free-for-all; we have to learn how to see the one Christ reflected in countless ways – if I'm allowed another musical analogy, we have to hear the tune to which all the variations relate.

Our holiness isn't a matter of achievement but of relatedness to Christ.

Likewise with the Church as 'holy'. As I've indicated, our holiness isn't a matter of achievement but of relatedness to Christ. We are holy because we stand in the holy place, where Jesus stands; we are rooted in heaven where the Son adores and gives himself in love to the Father. 'Where I am, there will my servant be', says Jesus in John's Gospel; and where he is is next to the Father's heart. When our lives are caught up into his, that is where we belong; and that is why we are 'holy'.

And the Church is 'catholic'. The word means 'universal', certainly, but it has many more resonances. It isn't just a geographical term – the Church was 'catholic' when it consisted of no more than twelve people in Jerusalem. One of the great writers of the fourth century explains that it also means that the Church tells the whole truth to the whole human race, to every sort of person. In Greek, the word meant something like 'of general application'. So a 'catholic' Church is one that is always concerned with wholeness – being faithful to the whole of its own treasury of faith, but also trying to relate to the whole variety of human experience, cultural and individual, confident in its capacity to speak the same truth to everyone in terms they can make their own. This creates many tensions, because it isn't always clear what is a proper adaptation and what is giving way to what is easy or fashionable. There is nothing new about that problem – it was around from the earliest days. Being catholic is being ready to live with the difficult job of discerning truthfully and with integrity in this area.

The 'apostolic' Church is one where we know we are here in virtue of the fact that the first disciples were *sent* (which is what the word 'apostolic' means). We believe, humanly speaking, because others took the trouble to come to where we are and invite us to belong with Jesus. We celebrate our continuity with them; but being apostolic doesn't mean just looking backwards – a mistake we have sometimes made. It is about recognizing the challenge now to share the same mission, to go where people are and invite them to come in. An apostle is a delegate, a spokesperson, someone sent on behalf of another. We are to be such delegates, learning how to speak not for ourselves but for Jesus.

All these features of the Church are visible only in pretty patchy ways when we look at the actual history of Christian communities. And we believe these things about the Church not because we have lots of evidence that this is how the Church is, but because of what we believe about Jesus. In a very important sense, all that we say about the Church is actually about Jesus. We are talking about *his* life and reality in the Church – and because that isn't dependent on how well or badly the Church is doing, we can say that it is always there, the true heart of what and who we are.

One of the simplest possible definitions of the Church is to say that it is meant to be the place where Jesus is visibly active in the world. And once we have said that, we can turn it around and say that where Jesus is visibly active, something very like the Church must be going on. This is very far from saying that the visible Church and its teachings and sacraments don't matter; it is simply to recognize that at times we learn something about what most matters in the Church by looking outside its visible boundaries. We see a form of behaviour that shows radical forgiveness or extraordinarily courageous hope, and we are able to say, 'Yes, *that's* it; that's the kind of thing I mean when I think about the Church and what it's for.'

And we can then perhaps look at the current state of the

Church we're in and ask some awkward questions about how we have let ourselves be distracted. We are in fact pushed back towards the centre of things, to Bible and sacraments, to the Christ whose life is still there at the heart of the community, so that we learn a bit of penitence. It's as if the power of Christ and the newness of the gospel always escape across the frontiers of the Church and come back to challenge the

The power of Christ and the newness of the gospel always escape across the frontiers of the Church.

Church from unexpected quarters. The Spirit is at work in creation, urging everyone towards Christlike behaviour and relation; sometimes, in 'uncovenanted' ways, it breaks through and we must have the humility to acknowledge it and learn from it. We have to grant that quite a lot of the concerns that modern Christians take for granted about human dignity, about liberty of conscience, about the evils of tyranny or the status of women, have been pressed upon the Church largely from outside its frontiers; and we have had to recognize, not that the Church is wrong and secular society is right, but that we have missed out on some basic and radical implications of our own language and practice.

So when we speak about those moments when we recognize the essence of the Church, we must accept that sometimes those moments are triggered by people and actions outside the Church itself. We might remember Jesus himself saying about the Roman centurion, who asks him to heal his servant, that he had not found trust as complete as this man's in the whole of Israel. But of course all such moments would be random and meaningless if we did not have the central story to tell of Jesus and his explicit call to follow him as part of a new community. So we cannot get away from the need to have narratives about the Church itself 'coming through' in its full richness. The silly journalist who went to Soviet Russia in the 1920s and came back saying, 'I have seen the future and it works' was grotesquely mistaken; but by God's grace we can sometimes say, 'I have seen the Church and it works.' We will all (I hope) have examples; here are a few that have helped me say it.

Back in the millennium year, the 'Jubilee 2000' campaign for debt relief reached a climax with a huge demonstration in Birmingham in the UK, where the economic power-brokers of the G8 countries had gathered. We had brought two coach loads from my diocese in South Wales; and, as I looked at the extraordinary variety of Christian groups on the streets – Catholic, Pentecostal, outrageously left-wing and outrageously right-wing – I, like others, felt able to say, 'I have seen the Church and it works.' Something of a real hunger and thirst for justice in Christ's name had drawn and held this unlikely coalition; its only agenda was to further what all believed was the call of God's kingdom, to resist what offended God's justice.

Jubilee 2000: witnessing for justice and debt relief

Or look at Penrhys, a remote hilltop council estate in the Rhondda Valley in South Wales, awash with social problems, the ultimate destination of some of the most challenging families from the nearby city of Cardiff, 'deported' there by local authorities at the end of their tether – with teenage pregnancy, third-generation unemployment, decayed housing and no routine social facilities. In the 1980s, a retired senior minister of the United Reformed Church and his wife decided to move to Penrhys, buying up two council properties, in one of which they lived, with the other becoming a mixture of drop-in centre, second-hand clothes shop and worship space. This space had been superbly designed, roomy and quiet, with simple furniture, an icon and a candle and no expectations, simply a place where people could be silent. Folk on the estate spoke of dropping in at the 'church' when they went to the shop and of using the 'chapel' while they were there; not a bad distinction to draw, since the whole complex was very clearly a church, a place where Jesus was visibly active. Before – at long last – the local authorities began to move people out from so obviously dysfunctional an environment, the church had also been a partner in the opening of a local health centre. It was, quite simply, the only focus in this community for some sort of dignity and care; a focus of trustworthiness in a context where trust was not much in evidence. 'I have seen the Church . . .'

Trust is at the heart of my third example. In recent years, the Solomon Islands in the Pacific have been troubled by severe outbreaks of violence between people from different islands. They are also the cradle of one of the most distinctive religious orders in the Anglican Church, the Melanesian Brotherhood –

totally committed to and identified with the local culture, innovative in its spirituality. In the conflicts in the islands, the Brothers remained one of the few groups to hold the trust of diverse factions, and their work for reconciliation was vital, and consistently brave. In 2003, seven of them were taken hostage by one of the factions and later killed in cold blood. It was one of the moments of traumatic realization that prompted moves towards peace, precisely because the islanders as a whole regarded the Brothers with such trust and love. Even more than my other examples, this displays something fundamental to the essence of the Church – its capacity to appear as (and to be) a community with no private interests to defend, reflecting something of God's own equal, free, non-partisan love. 'I have seen the Church . . .'.[10]

There is a saying from one of the monks of the desert in the early Church, a second-generation figure who observed sadly, 'I am not a monk, but I have seen monks.' He is aware of living in a somewhat compromised atmosphere; the first flame of enthusiasm has died down. But he knows what a true monk looks like, even if he knows that his own life is some way from that ideal. So also for us: when we have taken part in the sacramental worship of the Church and listened patiently to the Bible, we have seen the Church, even if by the next day we may feel we are no longer actively and visibly a Church. When we hear the stories of Penrhys or the Melanesian Brothers, we can say, 'Yes, we have seen the Church', even though it seems a long way from either the comfort or the confusion of our local Christian life. And these things are given us not so that we should feel guilty but so that we should feel grateful – even hopeful. God has not stopped making the Church to be the Church.

Blessed are the peacemakers . . . the murdered Brothers are brought home

In the sacraments and in the life of costly service, the same thing comes through: this is where the world in God's purpose is meant to be heading. This is the future, this is the sign of a 'peaceable kingdom', a realm in which God directs, shapes and draws the variety of human and non-human reality towards a state where humanity and the whole material world speak clearly of his glory. When the Church fails, divides, compromises, something has been lost of its conviction that it is there for the sake of God's future. And when the Church is fully itself, it is not because it has achieved a particular kind of human success, a high standard of behaviour, a statistically significant number of very saintly individuals, but because it has become transparent to God's future – the same thing, in effect, as being transparent to the indwelling life of Jesus.

But all this is steering us towards the final sections of the creeds. What is the future that God intends? And what do we do to collaborate with that intention – or to frustrate it?

Dᴀᴠɪᴅ Jᴏɴᴇs The Briar Cup (1932)

SIX

Love, Actually

I look for the resurrection of the dead

Life in the Holy Spirit is life where Jesus is alive in the company of others; life where each person, by the energy of the Spirit, gives the promise and possibilities opened up by Jesus to every other. So the Church, in which 'the fellowship of the Holy Spirit', as St Paul calls it, is a reality, is where everyone 'ministers' Jesus' reality. Each person becomes fully himself or herself in being the channel of Christ's action to the community – the believing community in the first place, but the whole community of creation as well.

So to say that the Church is where Jesus is visibly active in the world is to say both that it shows to the world the face of Jesus and that in its own internal life it embodies the life of Jesus, flowing between believers. And this takes us a little further. If the Church is where the life of Jesus is visibly active, it is the place where the life of the Holy Trinity is visibly active: the Spirit brings Christ alive in us, and that life is a life of adoration and self-giving directed towards God the Father. We certainly could not understand what matters most about the Church if we ignored the fact that Jesus' life is so directed. It was one of the oddities of the 'death of God' movement in the sixties of the last century that it professed an intense commitment to Jesus and the 'values' for which he stood, yet wanted to sidestep the central importance in all that we know about Jesus of his relation to the one he called 'Abba, Father'. And the same applies to anyone who says that they admire or respect or want to imitate Jesus but have difficulties about a transcendent God: it just is not possible to empty out of Jesus' story this constant, all-pervading, sometimes dark and agonizing, always decisive relation to the mystery out of which he comes.

To be in the Church is to be in the middle of that divine life, which Jesus uncovers for us – the outpouring and returning and sharing, gift and response and renewed overflow of giving, the threefold rhythm of love, Father, Son and Spirit. Those are the waves that surge around you as you try to live the life of discipleship, which is not the following of a distant figure in the past or simple obedience to a distant figure in the present, but participation in the rhythm that sustains the universe. When we think of life in the Church, perhaps we ought to think less in terms of signing up to a society and more in terms of swimming in an overwhelming current of divine loving activity; and, as we shall see a bit later, the same image helps us think more accurately about what's happening when we pray.

Where the Church is, there the action of the Holy Trinity is visible. Now, in recent theology many writers have made a good deal of the idea that the Church is 'the image of the Trinity'. It has provided a very fruitful way of seeing the Church as a balance of unity and plurality, or rather a unity that is indistinguishable from and constituted by the interwoven plurality of God's action; as a context where what makes me have an identity is always absolutely bound up with the otherness to which I am related. As in God's life, you can't say that unity comes before plurality or that diversity comes before harmony: they are completely simultaneous.

This has been a fruitful set of images and ideas. The only caution I have to offer is against thinking that God and the Church are two examples of life in 'communion'. We need to be clear that our life in the Church is what it is because we are taken up into the eternal reality that is God: the relationships of communion within the Church and with the rest of creation are the working-out of the gift that is given when the Spirit takes us into the heart of Jesus' prayerful relation to the Father. It isn't that God is a communion of three persons and the Church is a communion of several billion persons. The communion of human persons in the Church is something that is always being drawn more and more deeply into the absolute unity-in-difference that is God, though that unity-in-difference will always be beyond our grasp, and divine persons are never to be thought of as a bigger and better version of human persons.

However we set it out, the basic truth about the Church is clear. Its life points not only to Jesus Christ but to that rhythm, that interwoven knot of action and love within which Jesus stands, the threefold life that is God. 'Love, actually': this is where the eternal reality of selfless divine love and gift is to be identified in the world – not always (though sometimes) in the 'performance' of the Church, which so often is embarrassingly bad, but in the

When the Church is most clearly committed to the work of transforming the earth, heaven becomes most clear.

ritual and language of the Church, in the way the Church expresses what it believes it is. When this appears, in Holy Communion, in the gathering of people to hear and receive God's Word, in the faithfulness of some communities in Birmingham and the Rhondda and Melanesia and wherever else, what is going on is a sort of answer to the request in the Lord's Prayer – 'Thy will be done, on earth as it is in heaven.'

Or, to put it boldly, what we see is *heaven*. The Church has its roots in heaven, its real identity and dwelling-place in heaven – which is why St Paul says in his Letter to the Philippians that Christians have their 'citizenship' in heaven (Philippians 3.20). You might think back to chapter 3, and what was said there about Jesus inviting people into citizenship in a new world. Heaven is what is laid open when the Church is truly the Church. That's a rather counter-intuitive idea, perhaps, but it's what the Bible's picture of the Church suggests: not that the Church ceases to be really and concretely on earth, far from it; indeed, it is when the Church is most clearly committed to the work of transforming the earth in which it lives that heaven becomes most clear.

There is an old and well-known story about the conversion of the first Russian Christians in the tenth century. The envoys of the

Grand Duke of Kiev had visited various countries to examine the local religion; and when they arrived in Constantinople and attended the service in the great cathedral of Holy Wisdom there, they said, 'We did not know whether we were in heaven or on earth.' Quite right too: they had seen the Church and it worked; and what that meant was that they had been in heaven.

This may help to explain why in the creeds we move from expressing belief in the Church to affirming resurrection and eternal life. The Church makes sense only when we see that it exists to get us acclimatized to peace and praise, to bring us now into the atmosphere where what pervades and shapes everything is the life of God the Holy Trinity. So it's natural to move on to these declarations about our final destiny. But as we do, we should notice that we're not asked to declare a belief in 'eternal life' in general or in 'immortality'. In the Apostles' Creed this is most startling because we say we believe in 'the resurrection of the body' – or rather, in the original, 'the resurrection of the *flesh*'. If we have – as most of us do – a vague idea that religion commits us to believing in 'life after death', and that this involves a sort of shadowy reproduction of ourselves floating up towards the sky (remember all those cartoon images from childhood), this phrase gives a bit of a jolt. Do we actually want this particular lump of bone and fat and hair that we know so well to have an eternal future? And isn't there a hint of something, well, rather creepy about such language?

It is one of the hardest doctrines to state convincingly in the present climate. We are a fantastically materialistic society, but we often seem to have no innate respect for bodies, and to imagine that the body really is only the envelope for an identity created by the mind and the will (it's one reason we get into such a mess thinking about human embryos – a bodily human organism but with no trace of anything we could call a mind or a will, so we can readily jump to the conclusion that it can't have ordinary human 'rights'). Christian faith says that since God has come to encounter us in this world of material bodies, *as* a material body, and since God continues to use material things and persons to communicate who and what he is, we can't suppose that life with him will ever simply sidestep our material life. The Bible speaks rather seldom of life with God in heaven; it is more inclined to talk about a renewal of creation, 'a new heaven and a new earth', as in the last book of the Bible. Life with God, it seems, is life in a *world* that has something in common with the world we now inhabit.

This is where it gets difficult. Our imaginations set to work and we produce pictures of the new world, the world we'd really like to live in; only they seem so often to produce only embarrassing clichés. Look at those pictures of the new heaven and new earth that you sometimes see in the glossy publications of some religious sects that claim to explain the real meaning of the Bible to you: the painful truth is that they can't help looking like holiday brochures of the naffest variety. The path to thinking about eternal life is strewn with cowpats and elephant traps; yet there it is, in Bible and Creed: 'the resurrection of the flesh', the new world. How do we do justice to what the tradition demands and still avoid the pitfalls?

Perhaps we can start from first principles. We are who we are because we live in a context that makes us who we are – a human context but also a non-human environment. We've seen already that our relation to both community and material context is intrinsic to the life of faith, not an afterthought or a luxury. Our holiness is bound up with other people and with the things of the world. Our relation with God is made visible (or not, of course) in how we conduct these everyday relationships. So if we believe in life with God that does not just evaporate at our physical death, it must still be life in community and context, life in a world where all our relationships with things and persons are fully anchored in the Trinitarian love of God and fully transparent to that love.

God knows – literally – what that might mean. But that seems to be the nature of the challenge and the promise of our faith. The gospel treats us seriously, in our wholeness; it promises a new world and it directs us to the central story of a bodily saviour whose material flesh and bones are not left around in the world but raised and transfigured into

If God holds on to us through death, he holds on to every aspect of us.

something recognizably continuous with earthly life, yet dramatically different. The resurrection of Jesus and the hope of eternal life with God become the ground of a promise that, whatever exactly this means, God does not redeem us by making us stop being what we are – beings who live in community and context. If God holds on to us through death, he holds on to every aspect of us – not just to a specially protected, 'immortal' bit of us. Whatever life with God is, it is not something more abstract or more isolated than what we now know.

Gerard Manley Hopkins wrote a well-known poem, 'Nature's Bonfire', in which he puts side by side the fast-moving change and drift of the material world ('Cloud-puffball, torn tufts, tossed pillows') in which human lives come and go like other things ('nor mark/ is any of him at all so stark/ But vastness blurs and time beats level'), with the lightning flash of resurrection.

> In a flash, at a trumpet crash,
> I am all at one what Christ is, since he was what I am, and
> This Jack, joke, poor potsherd, patch, matchwood, immortal
>   diamond,
>   Is immortal diamond.

In our present life, the 'immortal diamond' is inseparably bound up with all the mixed and not very impressive stuff of human nature. And when resurrection arrives, it is not that all the rest falls away, but that the 'diamond' now takes in everything. It is not that the diamond is one bit of us that survives; the implication is that it is the precious possibility of relationship with God in the whole of our human nature.

And so those experiences of an anticipation of heaven that we have associated with 'seeing the Church' are important because they are quintessentially experiences of community and context. We may be – well no, we just are – quite unable to give a description of heaven, but we can say, 'It cannot be less than this.' People are sometimes rather shocked if you say that Christianity does not believe in the immortality of the soul; but in fact, while the Bible and the tradition talk about 'immortal' life, they don't assume that this deathless existence is something reserved for a part of us only, as if there were a bit of us that didn't have a future and a bit that did, the solid lumpy bit and the hazy spiritual bit. We have

We have a future with God as persons, no less.

a future with God as *persons*, no less. The life that is given us by God in our mortal and material relationships takes in all of that, and on the further side of death (which by definition we can't *imagine*) nothing is lost.

Our hope has nothing to do with some natural feature of our existence, a soul that has natural immortality. Although this came to be taken for granted in the early centuries of the Church and deeply affected much of what we are used to hearing on the subject, the hope described in the Bible is connected not to any aspect of our lives but to God's faithful commitment to the whole of what he has made. And, to be fair to earlier Christian generations, while they usually *did* assume the immortality of the soul, they never lost hold of the larger promise of resurrection. In the Middle Ages, you will find writers describing the frustration of the soul after death as it waits for the Last Judgement when it can be reunited to the body. We don't have to accept the rather convoluted theories they worked out in order to tidy this up; but we can recognize that they understood the hope of eternal life as hope for persons not ghosts.

And, as I've said, the key to this is – yet again – the belief in a *trustworthy* God. The pattern we have had before us all the way through these reflections, the story of a God who is totally committed to what he has made and loved and worked with, whose action and purpose are all directed towards our flourishing and healing, all of that fits completely with the vision of a God who will not let us go even on the far side of death. What he has made and, more significantly, has made his own in the loving action of Jesus, he will not abandon. Ultimately, Christians believe in eternal life not because they believe something about themselves as human (that they have an immortal element in them), but because they believe something about God. And if this belief in eternal life rests on what is made known about God, there is no special reason for Christians to be that concerned about 'evidence for survival' or psychical research. It may be very interesting in its way, it may sometimes be a sign of obsessive anxiety, it may dangerously distract from the real challenges of the gospel; but it doesn't have much to do with the biblical view of eternal life, which takes it for granted that the challenge is to respond honestly and repentantly and joyfully to the presence of God's truth in our midst here and now in the news about Jesus.

Honestly, repentantly and joyfully – not an easy trio. It isn't all obviously and immediately good news for us. We began thinking about the meaning of 'judgement' a while back; and before we get too enthusiastic over eternal life with God we ought to pause and think more about this. As we saw, the coming judgement of Christ is something we have to be aware of day by day, not a remote or mythical prospect in the future. Every day we have to become accustomed to the truth.

And what happens when all our defences against the truth are finally taken away? When we have to come to terms with God in some unimaginable dimension where our usual strategies of hiding from ourselves and the rest of reality are not available? How shall we manage being exposed to God and to our own consciousness as we really are? The New Testament already speaks of this in terms of 'stripping away' – St Paul can talk of our final destiny both as a frightening levelling of all we thought we had built or achieved (1 Corinthians 3.11–15, 2 Corinthians 5.1–5) and as a being clothed with a new 'covering' which is Christ's life (1 Corinthians 15.53–4, and the same passage from 2 Corinthians). Death means that something is removed that stands between us and God. But the hope is that if we have accustomed ourselves to living with Christ in this life something has been 'constructed' that allows us to survive the terror of meeting the truth face to face: the truth has come to be, in some degree, 'in us', to use the language of St John's first letter. At one level, we are left naked and undefended, with nothing of our own to appeal to or hide behind; yet we trust that we are gifted with the clothing, the defence we need.

It's no accident, then, that the ritual of Christian baptism in its most primitive form involved stripping and immersion and reclothing. The person who is entering the company of Jesus is letting go of defences, disappearing beneath the waters of death and emerging clothed in light and glory. Some of the most ancient Christian hymns from the Syriac-speaking world, the *Odes of Solomon*, regularly describe believers as clothed in light and crowned; they have 'put on Christ', in Paul's simple and powerful image (Romans 13.14).

Mortality and worldly pomp:
Archbishop Chichele's tomb in
Canterbury Cathedral

But, as Paul says in 2 Corinthians, before we put Christ on, we
have to have something taken off. In Canterbury Cathedral you
can see the fifteenth-century tomb of Archbishop Chichele: on the
top lies the Archbishop in all his ecclesiastical finery; underneath
is his naked corpse, ready for the worms. It is a sobering sight
(not only for Archbishops), a reminder that death is a nakedness
to which we must all come, a spiritual stripping, as we are confronted by God. The identities we have made, that we have pulled
around ourselves like a comfortable dressing-gown or a smart suit

will dissolve, and what is deepest in us, what we most want, what we most care about, will be laid bare. We are right to feel apprehensive about that, and we are wrong to brush away the sense of proper fear before God's judgement, however much we dislike the extravagant or hysterical expressions of it that have characterized some ages of Christian history. To the degree to which we don't know ourselves – a pretty high degree for nearly all of us – we are bound to think very soberly indeed of this moment of truth.

Death is a nakedness to which we must all come, a spiritual stripping, as we are confronted by God.

Yes, of course it's good that we have come some way from the situation where Christian rhetoric played on the fear of death and generated endless terrors and nightmares; it is a great distortion when faith is so mixed with anxiety. Yet there is a proper adult awareness of the fact that nakedness before God will hurt, because truth does hurt. Think of all the moments when you have realized, 'I've been deceiving myself, I don't understand why I did that, I did more damage than I allowed myself to know' – these are painful times. Even more painful are those moments when someone else sets out to show you to yourself and you want to hide, you want to shut them up. The Eastern Orthodox Liturgy asks for 'a good answer before the terrible judgement seat of Christ'. It is worth praying for, in the knowledge that such a 'good answer' can only be provided by the one who has promised to be our advocate, the truth in person.

A great theologian once said that the best justification for training clergy in residential settings was that living in community allowed you to say things to each other that still woke you up in a cold sweat thirty years later. Helping one another to see the truth about themselves is certainly part not only of training clergy but of the whole life of the Church, even though it is perhaps not to be embraced with quite the gusto exhibited by some – those who want to use 'speaking the truth in love' as a means of keeping others in their place! I'd rather think of the way in which a really holy person obliges us to see the truth, to see humanity for what it is and what it could be. Throughout these chapters I have returned several times to the impact on us of people who seem to be more naked to the truth than the rest of us. They help us believe; but they also can threaten us and make us react violently. It's a reminder that truth will hurt. Can there be any fallen human being who could face the prospect of confronting God's purity and light without shrinking?

It's this sort of thinking, of course, that lies behind the Catholic teaching about Purgatory. It has been a controversial subject in the Church since the Reformation, and the popular version of it deserved a lot of the opprobrium that the early Protestants directed towards it. Working off your debts until you become more or less worthy to go to heaven doesn't quite sit with the radical hopes of the New Testament, let alone the various ways in which the late medieval Church made a bit of a cottage industry out of securing grace for souls in Purgatory by organized sacramental 'lobbying' for them. But initially the impetus is surely the recognition that in our encounter with God, so long as we are the complex and self-deceiving beings we are, there will be a dimension of pain. We don't have to think about an intermediate state, a remand prison, but rather of a continuing journey with God as we become acclimatized to the fullness of love; or, to change the metaphor, something like our lungs expanding to cope with a new atmosphere.

The suggestion of a process or a period may not be helpful, even if it's unavoidable. Christian poetry comes closest. In Cardinal Newman's poem, *The Dream of Gerontius*, Gerontius, faced with God after death cries 'Take me away', and accepts the purification he must undergo simply by being in God's company. More gently and meditatively, George Herbert's well-known poem, *Love* (the third of that title) sets it out as a little drama: 'Love bade me welcome; yet my soul drew back.' Despite the welcome, we cannot believe we are meant to be here; love must tell us that he has made us and made us to be worthy. The immensity of the welcome forces us to know what we really merit –

> let my shame
> Go where it doth deserve.
> And know you not, says Love, who bore the blame?
> My dear, then I will serve.
> You must sit down, says Love, and taste my meat:
> So I did sit and eat.

What more is there to say in the wake of this, the greatest

Christian poem in the English language? The whole gospel is there, the realism about shame and guilt, the equal, heartbreaking realism about love overcoming every obstacle of self-hate, self-doubt and fear; the monosyllabic simplicity of the end. All there is to do is sit down with him at his table, just as Zacchaeus and Matthew and Magdalene and Peter knew.

But – 'Go where it doth deserve'? Where is that? What can we say about the punishment we have brought on ourselves – or is the gospel such that all this language can be left behind once and for all? We have had so much silly and downright wicked talk of hell in Christian history that it isn't surprising if we turn away in disgust from all the sadistic fantasies and emotional manipulation involved. But once again there is something we shouldn't write off. There is a proper adult awareness of the risk of our habitual unwillingness to face truth. What if throughout my life I made choices that made me more and more desensitized to truth, more and more incapable of opening my clenched fists in the presence of love? What if I made myself unable to tell truth from lies?

It has to remain a 'what if?' No one can know of anyone else how deeply they have made themselves unable to see the truth; no one knows if there is a state of self-deceit so profound that someone becomes eternally impervious to love. C. S. Lewis in his famous little work, *The Great Divorce*,[11] attempts to help us see what it might mean to be caught in an eternal trap, always having the possibility of accepting love, yet shrinking from the cost of change, or simply not able to understand the possibility because of long-ingrained habits of suspicion and selfishness. It is a chilling book; the more so once you realize that it is not about other people but about you.

And that is the point of thinking about hell. We cannot know if anyone is ever in such a condition, but we have to know the proper fear that the choices we make are capable of destroying us. Christian theology has commonly taught that hell is our decision, not God's (apart perhaps from the most extreme of sixteenth-century Calvinists, who held that God condemned some people even before the Fall of Adam – though even they would have said that those who went to hell did so because their lives made them incapable of living with God or of experiencing God in any way except as torment). We have made ourselves deaf to God's words; and the most truthful image we can have of hell is of God eternally knocking on a closed door that we are struggling to hold shut. What matters is that we are as aware as we can be of all those things that might bring us to such a state of terror and deception – bringing them now,

The most truthful image we can have of hell is of God eternally knocking on a closed door that we are struggling to hold shut.

today, before God's judgement and mercy. Which is why, of course, a Christian community doing its job is a community where people expect to be repenting quite a lot, and where the confident calling of others to repentance, which Christians enjoy so much, needs to be silenced by self-scrutiny and self-questioning before God.

But the miracle is that a repentant community, a community of people who are daily aware of their own untruthfulness and lack of love and are not afraid to face their failures, is a community that speaks profoundly of hope. The Church does not communicate the good news by consistent success and virtue – as we have noticed – but in its willingness to point to God; and repentance, which says that you don't have to be paralysed by failure, is thus one of the most effective signs of the Church's appeal to something more than human competence and resource. Perhaps we should add a fifth mark of the Church to the four in the Creed – a Church that is one, holy, catholic, apostolic and repentant.

One of the oddest things in our culture is that we seem to be tolerant of all sorts of behaviour, yet are deeply unforgiving. The popular media mercilessly display the failings of politicians and celebrities; attitudes to prisoners and ex-prisoners are often harsh; people demand legal redress for human errors and oversights. We shouldn't be misled by an easy-going atmosphere in manners and morals; under the surface there is a hardness that ought to worry us. And this means that when the Church in the Creed and (we hope) in its practice points us to the possibility of forgiveness, it is being pretty counter-cultural.

We seem to be tolerant of all sorts of behaviour, yet are deeply unforgiving.

Let's be clear, though – this is not a form of sentimentality, an easy compassion that costs nothing. When a Christian is asked whether he or she would 'forgive', let's say, a terrorist bomber, the answer should *not* be 'of course'. For one thing, it isn't for anyone to forgive someone who has injured another: it's for the victim to forgive. And forgiveness can't just be mandated as something to be done once and for all and straight away. Certainly, Christians are told to forgive each other, but they should know better than most how long a job it can be. They can say that it's possible; but God forbid that they should try to force the pace for someone whose hurts they don't know at first hand. Nor should forgiveness be confused with leniency or making light of an outrage. A person may be forgiven by their victim, yet it will still be right for them to serve out a sentence or in other ways have to deal with the consequences of an action.

No, forgiveness is the restoration of a relation – humanly, with the victim of an offence, great or small, but also a relation with God. To say, as we do in the Apostles' Creed, that we believe in the forgiveness of sins is to claim, not that offences don't matter, nor that things can easily be made all right again, but simply that even the worst of our failures cannot shut a door for God. Failure and hurt can be reclaimed, not by us but by God – and if it is possible for God, that makes it possible for us. It is yet another implication of the way we earlier defined God's 'omnipotence' – that there is no situation in which his presence cannot make some difference; yet he has given us the power to say no, even if he never will. A belief in the forgiveness of sins is a tough and difficult one, and yet it points more clearly than almost anything else to the glory and the liberty of God. William Blake, not the most orthodox of Christian poets, I know, wrote:

> Mutual forgiveness of each vice
> Opens the gates of Paradise;

and in that at least he was a witness to the orthodoxy of the Creed. When we are prepared to turn not only to God but to each other, in the confidence that something is possible; even on the far side of terrible hurt and alienation, the world becomes larger. Look around, and you see why this article of the Creed is perhaps the most necessary to proclaim today, locally, interpersonally, internationally.

But, as various hymns and prayers insist, we are not in the business of faith in order to escape hell; and in addition to repentance being an essential preparation for eternal life, we have to think also of adoration. If eternity as God purposes it for us is a world of joy in giving and receiving, awareness of the glory and generosity of God in all things, all held in the context of the giving and receiving and rejoicing that is the life of the Holy Trinity, our best preparation is getting accustomed to gift and joy, opening ourselves to vision. At the end of one of his greatest works, *The City of God*, St Augustine wrote about heaven as a context where 'we shall rest and we shall see, we shall see and we shall love, we shall love and we shall praise. Behold what will be at the end without end. For what other end do we have, if not to reach the kingdom which has no end.'[12] We need to acclimatize to this aspect of truth as well – not just the austerity of truth but its splendour and loveliness. Indeed, it is as we get used to the loveliness that we gather strength for the cost.

For the Christian tradition, eternity is above all a joy in the sheer reality of God – not an absorption in some final 'absolute' but a living relation, more like personal relation than anything else, yet somehow different because set in the heart of the exchange of life and joy within the Trinity. Eternity requires *contemplation*; a word that can make Christians panic a little from time to time – yet all it means is bringing ourselves into the light, beginning the process of acclimatizing to love, actually.

Eternity is above all a joy in the sheer reality of God.

It has been said that prayer is not primarily a matter of getting ourselves where we can see God so much as getting ourselves where God can see us – that is, getting ourselves into the light of his presence, putting aside our defences and disguises, coming into silence and stillness so that what stands before God is not the performer, the mask, the habits of self-promotion and self-protection but the naked me. But that's why the path of contemplation has always been seen as one of darkness as well as light. When we undertake to spend that sort of time in that sort of way before God, we undertake to let go of most of what usually makes us feel safe or good. The deepest challenge of the calling to contemplation, especially for those who make it a lifetime's work, is that it may never feel useful and readily justifiable. It's taken on not for a simple set of results but for the sake of truth, for the sake of eternity.

Like heaven itself, contemplation demands everything and gives everything; it is about stripping and it is about letting yourself more and more be clothed with Christ, taken into his prayer and love. As any contemplative will say, the Church is going to wither and dry up unless there are some who take on this calling in a public and evident way; monks and nuns and hermits are not picturesque extras in the Church but people who show something of its very heart and put into sharp perspective the fussiness of most of our plans and projects. The life given to this unsparing attention and focus on eternal joy is, paradoxically, one of the most utterly draining and demanding lives there could be; yet it shows what the truth is worth.

We have to pass through midnight before it turns towards dawn.

It means letting go of the images we are used to, moving beyond ideas and pictures of God that belong in our comfort zone. It means letting go of the emotions that we'd like to have, letting go of what we think makes us happy – not to cultivate misery but to get used to the idea that real joy might be so strange and overwhelming that we'd fail to recognize it unless we had put some distance between us and our usual comforts and re-assurances. At the prosaic and daily level, it can involve a great deal of sitting there facing frustration and self-doubt of the most acute sort: God calls me to delight and eternal fulfilment – so why exactly am I sitting here twiddling my thumbs, shifting from buttock to buttock, and wondering where, what and who God is?

Bit by bit, the props are being taken away. In the work of one of the very greatest masters of Christian contemplation, St John of the Cross in sixteenth-century Spain, the picture is of a journey into deeper and deeper darkness, a sense of being completely lost, imaginatively and emotionally. We face not only dryness and boredom but spells of desolation and fear that can be shocking in their intensity. As John says, we have to pass through midnight before it turns towards dawn. Only when the last traces of self-serving and self-comforting have been shaken and broken are we free to receive what God wants to give us. Only then shall we have made room for God's reality by disentangling God from all – or at least some – of the mess within our psyches. Prayer is letting God be himself in and for us.

Not many are called to the lifetime's work of the contemplative; but all believers *are* called to the same journey of letting God be himself for us. It's really an outworking of the first and second of the Ten Commandments – there shall be no other gods before the true God and no images to be worshipped in place of God. All of us to some degree use God to fill the gaps in our needs and preferences – which means that all of us are guilty of making images and putting false gods in place of the true one. God is God; he is not obliged to conform to our expectations. And because the reality is so immeasurably greater than any mind or heart or imagination can take in, we must let go in order to make room.

Once again, the Christian conviction about God as Trinity helps us to live with some of the puzzles here. Our calling is to be taken up into the relation of the eternal Son to the Father; but the life of the Trinity is not a case of external relationships between individuals – so that relation of intimacy and exchange is not going to be like one between human persons. We ought not to be surprised or wrongfooted if in our prayers we do not have the feeling that we are simply talking to another person just like us. If we are somehow included in Christ's relation to God the Father, it will not be as if we were relating to an individual on the other side of the room. Something is going on that is deeper than that, but no less personal, no less a real relationship, but something that doesn't depend entirely on how we feel and what we think: a pouring-in of God's love that will steadily transform us from inside. We are growing into mature life – growing into a grateful and secure awareness of ourselves that is always reaching out in what may feel like a blind love and searching for an Other beyond words and ideas, receiving always the influx of gift that makes us what we are, yet normally unable to say quite how this works. Praying in Christ, in the way a writer like St John of the Cross sketches it, is being carried on an invisible current of love that is sometimes discernible to us, but often (painfully) not. We can only trust that growth is happening; we know that it is happening only as we test our slowly expanding capacity to face truth, to accept our failures, to go on questioning ourselves because we trust that God will not let go of us.

In other words, the path of contemplative prayer is a working out of the whole vision we have been thinking about, the process that the creeds try to codify – moving deeper into trust as we discover what it means to be the object of an eternally trustworthy love. It is the outworking of what Martin Luther and his followers called 'justification by faith' – the belief that it is trust that sets you right, not achievement, success, performance, but the confidence that something has been shown and shared with us in the history that the Bible records which makes it possible for us to risk putting our hands into the hands of God. And when we pray, that is what we do; we put out our

When we pray . . . we put out our hands . . . into a darkness that is God's welcoming touch.

hands, as relaxed and open as we can make them, free, aware, without fantasies and projections, into a darkness that is God's welcoming touch.

When we say 'Our Father', when we come to God with Jesus' words on our lips and Jesus' Spirit in the depths of our being, trying to purge ourselves of all the things that just make us feel better or safer, when we step further towards the truth – then we understand what 'I believe' means. Then, in what the seventeenth-century poet Henry Vaughan called the 'dazzling darkness' of God, we start to become human in the fullest possible way. The work of a lifetime, but at the same time a gift that we have not earned and never shall. And let George Herbert conclude for us, telling us in his sonnet on prayer what it is we are secretly and slowly acclimatizing ourselves to:

> God's breath in man returning to his birth . . .
>> the soul's blood,
> The land of spices; something understood.

NOTES

1. T. S. Eliot, 'Little Gidding', *Four Quartets*, London, Faber & Faber, 1943.

2. St Ambrose, *De Fide* (On Belief), I.42.

3. *Etty: The Letters and Diaries of Etty Hillesum, 1941–1943*, ed. Klaas A. D. Smelik, Grand Rapids, Eerdmans, 2002, pp. 506, 640, 519.

4. Tony Hendra, *Father Joe: The Man who Saved my Soul*, London, Penguin Books, 2004.

5. *Father Joe*, pp. 191, 214.

6. *Father Joe*, p. 221.

7. Tom Stoppard, *Jumpers*, London, Faber & Faber, 1972.

8. See, for example, John V. Taylor, *The Christlike God*, London, SCM Press, 1992.

9. Kitty Ferguson, *The Fire in the Equations: Science, Religion and the Search for God*, West Conshohoken PA, Templeton Foundation Press, 2004.

10. See Richard Carter, *In Search of the Lost: The Death and Life of Seven Peacemakers of the Melanesian Brotherhood*, Norwich, Canterbury Press, 2006.

11. C. S. Lewis, *The Great Divorce*, London, Collins, 1945.

12. Augustine of Hippo, *City of God*, XXII.30.

ACKNOWLEDGEMENTS

The author and publisher acknowledge with thanks permission to use the following paintings by David Jones. Used by permission of Anthony Hyne for the Estate of David Jones:

page 2, The Waterfall, *Afon Honddu Fach* (1926)
page 30, The Annunciation, *Y Cyfarchiad I Fair* (1963)
page 56, A Man for All Seasons, *Sanctus Christus de Capel-y-ffin* (1925)
page 80, The Royal Banners, *Vexilla Regis* (1948)
page 104, The Farm Door (1937)
page 134, The Briar Cup (1932)

and the following photographs:

page 41, Lanzarote volcanoes by Richard King
page 50, London traffic by Rab Bower
page 70, Easter at the New Apostolic Church, South Africa, 2005
   © Chris Kirchhoff
page 86, Fleeing Basra © Caerdroia
page 96, Easter at Agio Thomas by Nicholas Econopouly at
   www.greecetravel.com/photos/sixties
pages 125 and 133, The Melanesian Brothers © Richard Carter, *In Search of the Lost*, Canterbury Press, 2006. Pictures by Carolyn Kitto (p. 125) and Richard Toke (p. 133)
page 130, Break the chains of debt © Jubilee 2000 Coalition
page 146, Tomb of Archbishop Chichele © P. E. Blanch 1998. Used by kind permission of the Dean and Chapter, Canterbury Cathedral